Elite • 150

World War I Gas Warfare Tactics and Equipment

Simon Jones • Illustrated by Richard Hook

Consultant editor Martin Windrow

First published in Great Britain in 1994 by Osprey Publishing,
Midland House, West Way, Botley, Oxford OX2 0PH, UK
44-02 23rd St, Suite 219, Long Island City, NY 11101, USA
Email: info@ospreypublishing.com

Osprey Publishing is part of the Osprey Group.

Transferred to digital print on demand 2009

First published 1994
13th impression 2008

Printed and bound by PrintOnDemand-Worldwide.com, Peterborough, UK

A CIP catalogue record for this book is available from the British Library

ISBN: 978 1 85532 361 2

Series Editor: Martin Windrow
Filmset in Great Britain by Keyspools Ltd, Golborne, Lancashire

Acknowledgements

The author wishes to express his thanks to the institutions which provided photographs for this volume: the National Museum
of Antiquities of Scotland, Edinburgh; the Ashmolean Museum, Oxford; the Museum of London; the British Museum; and
especially the German Archaelogocial Institute, Rome. I should also like to that the artist, Richard Hook, for his cheerful
patience in altering the colour plates specification every time I changed my mind; and to my wife, Kati, who drew the map
and lived with the Guard much longer than it was reasonable to expect of her.

Artist's note

Readers may care to note that the original paintings from which the colour plates in this book were prepared are available
for private sale. All copyright whatsoever is retained by the publisher. All enquiries should be addressed to:

Scorpio Gallery,
PO Box 475
Haillsham
East Sussex
BN27 2SL

The publishers regret that they can enter into no correspondence upon this matter.

The Woodland Trust

Osprey Publishing is supporting the Woodland Trust, the UK's leading woodland conservation charity, by funding
the dedication of trees.

www.ospreypublishing.com

WORLD WAR I GAS WARFARE TACTICS & EQUIPMENT

INTRODUCTION

Although chemical warfare was outlawed at the 1899 Hague Conference, after the Russo-Japanese War of 1904–5 France, Germany and Britain all experimented with tear-gases – which they did not consider to be a violation of the Hague agreements. From September 1914, the search for ways of breaking the stalemate of trench warfare caused them to turn again to chemical weapons, and the French used tear-gas cartridges developed before the war from weapons used by the Paris police. In early January 1915, Gen Curmer, head of the technical section of the French corps of engineers, ordered another design of tear-gas hand grenade, designed by Prof Gabriel Bertrand of the Pasteur Institute and Sorbonne.

In Britain in late 1914, Profs Herbert Baker and Jocelyn Thorpe tested about 50 possible substances in a trench dug at Imperial College in South Kensington, London. By January 1915 they had identified ethyl iodoacetate as an effective tear-gas which did not corrode a metal container. When the effects on a tall War Office official were inconclusive, a boy was offered a shilling to enter the trench, settling the question. The substance was named SK after the location of the trials (South Kensington). A grenade resembling the so-called 'jam tin' pattern of high explosive grenade was tested at Chatham; and in March 1915 a 4.5in howitzer shell was tested at Shoeburyness.

A German attempt to increase the effect of 10.5cm shrapnel shells by adding an irritant – dianisidine chlorosulphonate – went unnoticed by the British when tried at Neuve Chapelle in October 1914. Hans Tappen, a chemist in the Heavy Artillery Department of the War Ministry, suggested to his brother, the Chief of the Operations Branch at German General Headquarters, the use of the tear-gases benzyl bromide or xylyl bromide. Shells were tested successfully at the Wahn artillery range near Cologne on 9 January 1915, and an order was placed for 15cm howitzer shells, designated 'T-shells' after Tappen. A shortage of shells limited the first use against the Russians at Bolimov on 31 January 1915; the liquid failed to vaporize in the cold weather, and again the experiment went unnoticed by the Allies. The Germans then added bromacetone to the agent, and used the shells against the French on the Belgian coast in March.

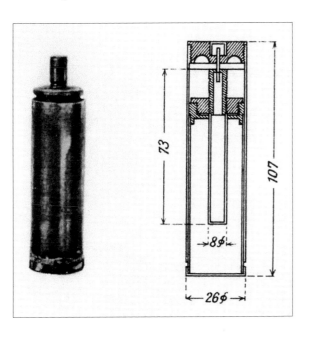

The first chemical weapon of the war: the French 26mm *cartouche suffocante* rifle grenade, fired from a flare carbine. It contained 35g of the tear-producer ethylbromacetate, and was used in autumn 1914 – with little effect on the Germans. A larger version was in use from February 1915. (From *Die Feindliche Gasmunition*, January 1918: REM)

73
107
8⌀
26⌀

The shell shortage led Prof Fritz Haber, Director of the Kaiser Wilhelm Institute for Physical Chemistry, to suggest releasing chlorine gas from industrial cylinders. The French use of *cartouches suffocantes* persuaded them that they were justified morally in using both tear-gas shells and chlorine gas from cylinders, since it could be argued that neither violated the specific letter of the Hague agreement. In January 1915, Gen von Falkenhayn, Chief of the German General Staff, approved trials, and Prof Haber was placed in charge of the operation, code-named 'Disinfection'. On 25 January the decision was taken to make the attack on the Belgian Flanders front, on the southern part of the salient formed by the town of Ypres.

A gas Pioneer unit of 500 men was formed under Col Otto Peterson, initially called the *Pionierkommando* or *Disinfektionstruppe Peterson*; this was later expanded to a strength of 1,600, and designated Pioneer Regiment 35. German headquarters requisitioned 6,000 large commercial gas cylinders each holding 88lb of chlorine, and ordered 24,000 half-size cylinders containing 44lb of the gas. During February, Peterson's men began – with the help of infantry carrying parties – the dangerous job of installing the cylinders, which were 4–5ft high and weighed about 187lb, in the front line south of Ypres. Some were burst by Allied shellfire, and the escaping chlorine killed two men and injured fifty. By 10 March work was complete;

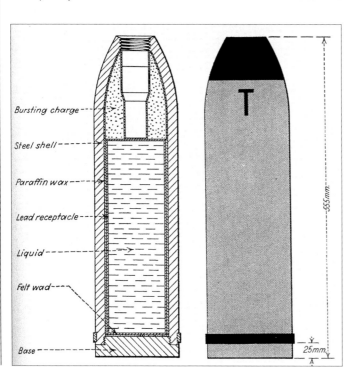

Bursting charge

Steel shell

Paraffin wax

Lead receptacle

Liquid

Felt wad

Base

T

555mm

25mm

but the Pioneers waited in vain for a favourable wind until, realizing that they had chosen the wrong location, they prepared a new site facing Ypres from the north. By 11 April, 1,600 large and 4,130 small cylinders, totalling about 340 tons of chlorine, were in place opposite the positions held by the French 87th Territorial and 45th Algerian Divisions. The release was twice postponed because of unfavourable winds, and the reserve troops earmarked to follow up the attack had to be withdrawn for the Gorlice-Tarnow offensive on the Eastern Front. The attack was to be delayed four more times, while the assaulting infantry remained packed in the trenches all day in readiness.

YPRES, SPRING 1915

At 5pm on the afternoon of 22 April 1915, with a loud hissing, jets of chlorine merged to form clouds in front of the German trenches, and drifted towards the French lines. As the puzzling greenish-yellow clouds reached the French trenches and revealed their nature, the defenders fled. The German infantry advanced, and since the French lines were thinly held, with no defence in depth and field artillery close behind, the front line was quickly overrun. In a few places the German troops were held up, especially by Belgian and Canadian troops on their flanks, where the gas was still hanging around. Nearly everywhere on that sector, however, the French front line was deserted: in the words of a German officer, 'the enemy had run away like a flock of sheep', and scores of French dead lay immediately behind their lines.

A French trench at Poelcapelle captured in the first gas attack on 22 April 1915. Gas victims were described as lying on their backs with their fists clenched. Exposure to chlorine gave a blue cast to the face and lips.

British victims of the chlorine attack at Hill 60 on 1 May 1915, photographed the following day at No.8 Casualty Clearing Station, Bailleul, where they were laid in the open to ease their breathing. The bowl is for fluid discharged from the lungs. Of 17 gas victims who reached this CCS, only three survived. The diary of SgtMaj Ernest Shepherd of B Coy, 1st Dorsets – a notably tough-minded pre-war Regular – reveals the troops' shock and fury on their first encounter with gas. The Dorsets had been warned against it, but believed it 'was to stupefy only. We soon found out at a terrible price that these gases were deadly poison... The scene that followed was heartbreaking... When we found our men were dying from fumes we wanted to charge, but were not allowed to do so... Had we lost as heavily while actually fighting we would not have cared as much, but our dear boys died like rats in a trap... The Dorset Regiment's motto now is, "No Prisoners".' (National Archives WO142/99)

Chlorine kills by irritating the lungs to such an extent that they flood with fluid, and the victim 'drowns'; gas victims show blueness of the lips and face as the blood becomes starved of oxygen. Between 800 and 1,400 men were killed in this attack, and another 2,000–3,000 injured. Many thought that the Germans could have made a more ambitious advance, had they correctly anticipated the effects of their attack and kept the required reserves in readiness. However, the operation proved that a mass infantry attack behind a gas cloud was impossible, as the right wind direction could not be guaranteed in advance to allow time for the necessary concentration of troops.

Allied protection attempts
The Allies had received warning of the attack from German deserters, and one even had a respirator in his possession; word of the manufacture of these had also reached Belgian intelligence. The information was circulated among the Allied troops in the Ypres Salient, but there was little grasp of what such an attack would mean, and it was assumed that the effects would be very local. No effort was made to arrange protection before 22 April.

On 23 April the French War Minister ordered Dr André Kling, director of the Paris municipal laboratory, to investigate the attacks; and Kling and Prof Bertrand were asked by Gen Curmer to devise a respirator. They had two types of German respirator to examine, and Dr Kling chose the simpler type as a pattern. General Curmer organized manufacture by seamstresses of the Paris department stores but, because the gas had not been definitely identified, no neutralizing solution was adopted; the masks were to be damped with water alone. On 24 April it was decided to produce 100,000 examples, and French armies were instructed to arrange for their own manufacture of masks to the same design.

On 25 April, Dr Kling arrived in Ypres and identified the gas as chlorine. A report from a pharmacist at the front identified the impregnation of a German mask as a mixture of sodium hyposulphite ('hypo', commonly used for developing photographs) and fixed alkaline hydrate in a glycerine solution, and these details were immediately sent to all armies. On the 28th, Gen Curmer convened a meeting of experts including representatives from the chemical industry, at which he required them first to consider reprisals. They also increased the order for respirators to one million, to be distributed as quickly as possible. Mine rescue oxygen breathing apparatus was ordered for key personnel such as machine-gunners and officers, and all such apparatus in the country was ordered to be sent to Paris. On the evening of the 30th the first were sent to the Tenth Army, along with 2,800 *grenades suffocantes* and 3,500 Bertrand grenades.

General Headquarters of the British Expeditionary Force (GHQ BEF) issued its first instructions concerning protection on 23 April. The British believed the gas to be chlorine, and instructed that field dressings should be soaked in bicarbonate of soda for use as respirators. A cloth dipped in an alkaline solution, such as urine, could be used to neutralize chlorine, and plain water would also have some effect. When no respirators arrived from the rear, many units took matters into their own hands. The 27th Division at Ypres arranged for lint strips with tying tapes to be made by nuns at Poperinghe Convent, and 3,000 were sent to the trenches by the following evening.

The Germans carried out a smaller attack at 2am on 24 April against the 1st Canadian Division, which had held out on the right flank of the French. That night about 15 tons of chlorine drifted as a dense, compact cloud over the cool earth of No Man's Land. The 8th Bn (Winnipeg Rifles) had only handkerchiefs and cotton bandoliers for protection – the initiative of Sgt Harry Knobel – to be held over the mouth after wetting from dixies of water. Breathing through damp cloths could remove sufficient of the chlorine to prevent men from collapsing, but only if it was diluted while drifting from the German lines. Major Matthews described

Well-known study of extemporized respirators worn by men of the 2nd Bn Argyll & Sutherland Highlanders in the Bois Grenier sector, May or early June 1915. They hold bottles containing hypo solution for wetting their pads. In III Corps, south of Ypres, the issue of the useless cotton wool *'Daily Mail* respirators' on 3 May so alarmed a chemist serving with the 1st Cameronians, Lt Leslie Barley, that he devised his own mask in a school science laboratory in Armentières. This was of cotton waste soaked in hypo in a muslin container secured with tapes. Wearing it, he cleared a chlorine-filled room with a hypo solution from a hand-pumped crop sprayer. In a few days 80,000 respirators were made up in local villages and convents, and sprayers were put in the trenches. (IWM Q48951)

a greenish-yellow wall of vapour at least 15ft high, which enveloped his men in less than three minutes. Many were overcome, but most managed to man the trench parapet: 'Men were coughing, spitting, cursing and grovelling on the ground and trying to be sick' (National Archives CAB45/156). By standing fast, and not running with the drifting clouds, the Canadians improved their chances of survival, since the gas soon passed behind them; but eventually the effects of the chlorine and shelling forced them from their trenches.

On 26 April, GHQ issued instructions on the advice of an Intelligence Corps officer, Lt George Pollitt, a industrial chemist who had just returned from organizing a spy network in Zurich. He suggested a folded square of flannel wetted with water, or even a handkerchief rolled into a ball and held in the mouth.

The Secretary of State for War, Lord Kitchener, summoned Prof John Haldane, an expert on gas poisoning and the discoverer of the cause of the 'bends' suffered by divers when ascending too rapidly. Winston Churchill, the First Lord of the Admiralty, had suggested that small cotton wool mouth pads used during Navy smokescreen experiments might be used as respirators. Haldane advised that these were of no use, because cotton wool cannot be breathed through once wetted with a neutralizing solution. Nevertheless the War Office followed Churchill's suggestion of making an appeal through the *Daily Mail* for the public to make up this mask, and another consisting of a small piece of stockinet. This appeared on 28 April under the headlines: 'Rush Job for Women – Respirators for Our Troops – All Homes Can Help'. The following day the War Office announced that 30,000 had been made and no more were needed. The *Daily Mail* respirators were useless, but many found their way to the front despite an assurance to Haldane that none would be sent.

On 1 May, the Germans released chlorine from 60 cylinders for a local attack on Hill 60 south of Ypres, where some of the trenches were only 20 yards from the German front line. In the early evening one company of 1st Bn Dorsetshire Regt were in the act of wetting the cloths issued in accordance with Pollitt's instructions, and another were waiting for water to arrive, when they were swamped with gas. Many immediately began choking and collapsed to the trench bottom, where the gas – being heavier than air – sank to envelop them. Most men found the cloth strips ineffective. One officer tried to use a piece of rifle flannelette until, when he was on the point of collapse, he tried a handkerchief well soaked in water, which enabled him to carry on until 6am. He and another officer rallied the few remaining men of his company, forcing them to mount the firestep and keep firing, which prevented the Germans from attacking. They remained clear of the gas in the bottom of the

The War Office Black Veiling Respirator, May 1915. These masks, soaked in a hypo solution, saved hundreds of lives during the chlorine attack of 24 May 1915. The eye flap is not apparent here. A waterproof pouch prevented it from drying out while not in use. (REM RSME0390070)

The Hypo Helmet. The first examples were made of standard Army grey shirting flannel. When stocks of this ran short, wool/cotton mixtures, such as Viyella, were used and khaki dye was added to the impregnating solution. This helmet was issued to Sgt David Forgan, 10th Bn Gordon Highlanders, who took part in the battle of Loos. The satchel, on which Forgan has written his initials, was introduced on 5 August 1915. (REM RSME0390070)

trench, and the cloths were sufficient protection to allow many to continue to fight. When the wind changed the Germans suffered casualties from their own gas. The Dorsets' defence was the first gas attack in which the Germans failed to take trenches, but their losses were severe: in C Company only 38 men were left on their feet.

On 2 May the Germans released gas on a three-mile front against nine British battalions; losses were heavy – the men had only pieces of flannelette, woollen waistbands or futile *Daily Mail* respirators. Once again, the defenders inflicted heavy losses on the Germans, who failed to take any trenches; but on 5 May they captured Hill 60 by means of two further gas attacks.

A German prisoner had been taken on 27 April with a respirator, and Prof Baker, sent out with Haldane to investigate the attacks, brought it home for testing and mass production. Baker designed a pad of cotton waste soaked with sodium hyposulphite, sodium carbonate and glycerine, held in gauze, which would protect against chlorine, bromine, sulphur dioxide and nitrous fumes. The cotton waste allowed air to pass through the pad while the gas was chemically neutralized by the salt solution. Baker added an eye-flap, and cut the gauze into 18in lengths, turning up the lower third and forming a pocket in the centre with two vertical lines of stitching. The ends of the gauze were tied behind the head, avoiding the need to sew on tapes. He chose black mourning gauze (for its availability), and the design became known as the Black Veiling Respirator.

Immediate manufacture was sanctioned on 3 May, but when Haldane returned from France two days later he discovered that orders had only just been placed. The pharmaceuticals firm Bell, Hills & Lucas Ltd began continuous production, which was only halted by an accident when caustic soda was mistaken for sodium carbonate, causing burns and bleeding to the hands of the women dipping the respirators.

By early May a handful of scientists in the BEF had been gathered in a high school science laboratory at GHQ. They included Lt Leslie Barley, a chemist who was serving with the 1st Cameronians; Bernard Mouat-Jones (Baker's former assistant professor, now serving as a private in the London Scottish), and a medical officer from the Newfoundland Regt, Capt Cluny MacPherson. They were well aware of the limitations of the Black Veiling Respirator: it was difficult to tie over the mouth in a hurry, gas leaked around the edges, and it gave protection for only a short time. Testing masks on themselves, they all suffered chlorine injury.

An early French hypo *Compresse*. The goggles were impregnated with castor oil, and were proposed by Prof Gabriel Bertrand in August 1915. (IWM Q61056)

MacPherson produced a flannel bag soaked in hypo, with a mica window, which completely enclosed the wearer's head. It was easy to put on, solved the problem of gas leakage and protected for longer. In London it was accepted as superior to the Black Veiling Respirator, but the latter was given priority owing to the time that would be lost if production was reorganized. MacPherson's mask became known as the 'Hypo Helmet', although in Army orders it was referred to as the 'Smoke Helmet'. Hypo Helmets began to arrive in France on about 8 May, and were distributed at a ratio of 1,000 per division. Many of the mica widows cracked because of hot air used in the drying process, and were replaced by triacetyl cellulose, but the problem was never adequately solved. Hand-operated Vermorel crop sprayers were also issued, used with hypo solution to neutralize the chlorine gas that gathered in trenches.

The real test of the Black Veiling Respirator came on 24 May, when a massive chlorine attack was made against the Ypres Salient. The volume and density of gas far exceeded British fears, and at least 46 battalions were exposed over a front of four and a half miles. Gas enveloped trees and houses three miles behind the lines, and was smelt six miles away. The anti-gas measures were incapable of saving all those in danger; not everyone had received the Black Veiling Respirator and only a few the Hypo Helmet. The wind was no more than a breeze, and the gas took about 45 minutes to pass over the trenches – the respirators worked for about five minutes before needing to be re-dipped. In the 2nd Royal Dublin Fusiliers, officers had to compel men to squeeze their respirators dry after re-dipping so that they could be breathed through, finding badly gassed men blue in the face and vomiting. The Germans captured trenches at Shell Trap Farm and around Bellewaarde Lake, but further advance was prevented by British machine gun and artillery fire not silenced by the gas. The following day the Second Battle of Ypres drew to a close. The effects of the gas appalled the British, and an exaggerated view of its military effectiveness was strongly to influence their plans for retaliation.

* * *

The issue of respirators to the larger and more widely spread French forces took nearly three weeks after 22 April, but fortunately they were spared gas attacks during this period. The first 150,000 French respirators made up in Paris were issued on 12 May to the Northern Army. The previous day an interim instruction was issued for troops who had yet to receive respirators, telling them to soak hay or other vegetable fibres in water for several hours and wrap them in a handkerchief. It was decided to copy the British Black Veiling Respirator and Hypo Helmet after a favourable report from the military attaché in London, Col de la Panouse. Doctor Kling visited the scene of the attack of 24 May; he reported that all troops should be issued with pads or Hypo Helmets, and that the French pads should be larger. From 27 May their size was increased to 5in x 10.5in, and oakum was used in the absence of cotton waste.

The respirator was named the *Compresse*, the new design being the C2. The tapes were replaced with a broader band, narrowing towards its ends, like the black veiling type, and a wire framework kept the filling evenly spaced. Some of the *Compresses* had methyl orange added as an indicator – this turned red when the absorbent was exhausted. After some delays, by the middle of August 1915 more than a million had been issued. In London, Panouse was asked to order 33,000 yards of khaki Viyella fabric for Hypo Helmets, while other fabrics were tested. The first 8,000 French Hypo Helmets were despatched on 21 May to the Northern Army, and 40,000 to the other armies the following day. The helmets were well received at the front, in particular for their ease of putting on. However, an order for two million helmets led the British to refuse to deliver Viyella for fear of having insufficient for their own needs. This led to variations of fabrics and designs of Hypo Helmets as they were produced by contract and by local orders from the individual armies.

The German gas troops now shifted to the Russian front, for a series of cloud attacks that started on 31 May. The first caught the Russians during a relief – i.e. while units were in the process of replacing one another, a time of crowding and relative confusion. This caused as many

Officer cadets train while wearing the P Helmet, and armed with Long Lee Enfield rifles, in practice trenches at Purfleet, 1915.

11

as 5,000 casualties, although a German reconnaissance in force was hit by unexpected resistance, and a wind change left 56 German gas casualties. During the second attack on 12 June the gas again blew back, causing 350 German casualties; worse was to follow on 6 July, when no fewer than 1,450 Germans were gassed of whom 130 were killed.

From May 1915 the German artillery began to use new gas tactics and chemicals against the French. They fired concentrated T-shell bombardments, which rendered the French trenches untenable – but were themselves unable to occupy them. At the opening of their Argonne offensive on 20 June 1915 they fired up to 25,000 T-shells, creating a white cloud against which the *Compresse* was ineffective; when Dr Kling visited three days later he found it impossible to remain in the area. He discovered that trench mortar bombs had been sent over containing bromine, a dense, red-brown vapour which irritated the eyes and respiratory tract. The French *Compresse* protected against inhaled bromine but did not protect the eyes, which were severely irritated by even low concentrations. Ten days later the Germans repeated the process, capturing 3,000 prisoners and forcing the French to withdraw from their positions.

On 16 July the Germans used chlormethylchloroformate (called by them *K-* or *C-Stoff*), a lung irritant more poisonous than chlorine and with serious tear effects. They again captured a large number of prisoners, but failed to follow up. Doctor Kling identified a sample of the chemical, naming it *Palite.* The Germans tried various other tear-producers, including bromacetone *(B-Stoff)* in July and brommethylethyl ketone *(Bn-Stoff)* in August, and took 5,000 prisoners at St Mihiel.

The British P Helmet

The worst fear of the Allied scientists was that the Germans would attack with a gas far more lethal than chlorine against which their respirators would be of no use. Research in the UK was centred at the Royal Army

Medical College at Millbank, London, under the direction of an Army professor of hygiene, LtCol Percy S.Lelean. From the list of gases that the Germans might use – which at one point exceeded 70 – two emerged as posing the most serious threat: phosgene, and hydrogen cyanide. The solution most favoured by the scientists, of layers of filtering materials in a box, was rejected by the Army as too great a departure from the design already in production, which would cause dangerous delay. The search was therefore on for a chemical that could be added to the Hypo Helmet to protect against a range of gases.

An apparatus was devised at Millbank to bulk-test protective chemicals on rats. If the rats survived, first a pig, and then a human volunteer, would test the helmet. All of the scientists were themselves poisoned during this work. Baker kept in correspondence with Mouat-Jones at GHQ at St Omer, and they simultaneously discovered a crucial protective chemical, sodium phenate. Baker discovered it during experiments at his home in which he inhaled phosgene and chlorine through an impregnated cloth held over his mouth. A 'Phenate Helmet' was tested at Millbank and was found to keep out both phosgene and hydrogen cyanide.

The new helmet was made from two layers of cotton flannelette, because the woollen flannel of the Hypo Helmet was rotted by the corrosive phenate. The window was replaced by two circular glass eyepieces in pressed tin rims. Carbon dioxide reduced the effect against hydrogen cyanide, so a valve was fitted through which the wearer breathed out – hence the name 'Tube Helmet' in Army orders. Opposition to the valve was overruled: definite intelligence was received of a German gas so lethal that Allied masks would be useless. Phosgene was strongly suspected, and the Phenate or 'P' Helmet was adopted as the new British gas helmet. By mid-November 1915 the issue of one per man was complete, and the Hypo Helmet carried as a reserve was being replaced by a second P Helmet.

BRITISH RETALIATION: LOOS, SEPTEMBER 1915

British preparations for their first gas attack were hasty, and overestimated the value of cloud gas to an infantry attack. On 26 May, LtCol Charles H.Foulkes, Royal Engineers, was appointed to command British gas troops. At Runcorn on 4 June he witnessed a chlorine discharge, and was impressed by the ability of the gas to cling to the ground and sink into trenches. He reported that 'such a cloud could be followed up safely in the open by unprotected infantry a minute or two after the discharge ceased'; but a 20mph wind was blowing – too fast for a cloud attack, since the gas would be too quickly dispersed to affect the enemy. Nevertheless, Foulkes' overconfident report led to preparations for a British gas attack; and between June and September four 'Special Companies Royal Engineers' were formed.

General Sir Douglas Haig, commanding the First Army, incorporated gas into an attack that he had been ordered to undertake at Loos in support of a major French offensive. He was pessimistic about the attack, but began to see possibilities with gas if the German success of

22 April could be duplicated and properly exploited. On 22 August a demonstration in the presence of Haig again seemed to confirm confidence in its potential. Haig was warned not to rely on gas for the success of his attack owing to the unpredictable nature of the wind, but on the morning of the attack he was unable to cancel when the wind changed. The 80 battalions of assaulting infantry were told that their gas helmets would give them a decisive advantage over the Germans, and that they should take full advantage of the surprise from the gas. In many cases the infantry who laboured night after night carrying the cylinders into the front line were the same men who immediately afterwards had to make the attack.

The gas was released from 5.40am until Zero Hour at 6.30am, 25 September, from 5,900 cylinders (see Plate B). Smoke bombs (or 'candles') were used to increase the apparent duration of the gas release to 40 minutes, because it was believed that German machine-gunners were equipped with Dräger oxygen breathing apparatus which only lasted for 30 minutes (see Plate A). Smoke was also fired from a new type of mortar; Foulkes had seen this demonstrated in July 1915, and had asked the inventor for a larger version for gas. Twenty-nine 4in Stokes mortars fired 10,000 smoke bombs improvised from papier mâché tubes filled with phosphorus; they were also fired from catapults and other mortars.

The gas and smoke caused panic behind the German lines, and the town of Loos was captured. However, in many places the chlorine gathered a few yards out in No Man's Land, and drifted northwards or back over the British trenches packed with troops. Although the German Hohenzollern Redoubt was swept with gas this also affected the trenches of the British 1st Division, and attackers had to form up in gas and smoke. Foulkes ordered that his personnel alone should be responsible for determining whether the wind was right, but several were overruled by staff officers, including one who was told that he would be shot if he did not release his gas. The variety of cylinders meant that the correct spanners were not always available, and the joints of the rigid lead pipes leaked gas into the British trenches. The discharging gas caused the valves to freeze, and the Special Company corporals could not turn them off. Thousands of infantry, laden with equipment and preparing to attack, found their trenches filled with chlorine from leaking cylinder pipe joints.

The British gas helmets also caused confusion. Although instructions stated that Hypo Helmets were to be worn for the attack in preference to the new P Helmets, many men wore the latter. These were rolled on the head ready to pull down; the weather was wet,

A Special Company RE member wearing a P Helmet demonstrates gas discharge at Helfaut, near GHQ BEF, in September 1915, just prior to the first British attack at Loos. Some of the flexible armoured hose seen here was available, but rigid lead pipes were mostly used; both had to be removed and reconnected as each cylinder was emptied.
(REM 6911-03)

A German Jäger and an infantry officer charge with grenades wearing the *Linienmaske*. This type and the *Rahmenmaske* are known collectively as the *Gummimasken* or 'rubber masks'. The infantryman has a Mauser C96 pistol at his hip in its wooden holster-stock, and appears to be brandishing the bayonet which by 1915 had usually replaced the officer's sword.

and the chemicals in the cloth, leeched out by the rain, irritated the skin and eyes. Both types of helmet were intensely stuffy for the first ten minutes of wear, and men forgot to breathe out through the tube valve, which aggravated this effect. Men lifted the helmets to get some fresh air, and inhaled chlorine. Many mistook the extreme discomfort of the helmets, their strong chemical smell and the irritation of their throats for gas penetrating the fabric.

Battalion medical officers were inundated with men in a state of panic, either gassed or only under the impression that they were. (One stated that the only difficulties to respiration were caused by the speed at which men had run to his dressing station.) Doctors also had insufficient experience of gas poisoning to distinguish it from symptoms of fatigue, exposure and shock. A study by the physiologist Dr Claude Douglas in 1918 concluded that, of 2,632 British soldiers evacuated as gassed following the 25 September attack, 1,696 were very slight cases and many not gassed at all.

British cloud gas attacks followed on 26 September and the last day of the battle, 13 October, without successful advance. Condemnation of both the ineffectiveness of the gas and the helmets was widespread after the battle. Moreover, five days before the Loos attack the BEF Army Chemical Advisers had been unanimous that P Helmets did not protect against high concentrations of chlorine. Later in the year the head of the GHQ Central Laboratory discovered that testing of helmets at Millbank had been carried out on a machine giving inaccurate readings.

MASKS & HELMETS, 1915–16

The German 1915 *Gummimaske*

In autumn 1915 the Germans introduced an advanced and versatile respirator. Doctor Bernhard Dräger, whose company made breathing apparatus, developed a light rubberized face mask with a metal drum containing filter materials at the 'muzzle'. He designed a facepiece to cover the mouth, nose and eyes, made from gas-impermeable cotton developed by Dr Hans Pick of the Kaiser Wilhelm Institute (although the first batch reportedly used fabric from the French airship *Alsace*, brought down near Rethel on 3 October). The eyepieces were made from shatterproof celluloid, soon replaced by a flameproof type; and the facepiece included two large folds which enabled the wearer to wipe condensation from the inside of the eyepieces. To ensure an airtight seal, the joins to the eyepieces and the filter attachment were bound with linen thread and all seams were lacquered. Flexible elasticated tapes from the temples to the back of the head held the facepiece firmly in place. A carrying tape enabled the mask to be hung in readiness on the chest. This design required an effective seal to the lines of the face for all shapes and sizes of head, hence it was known as the *Linienmaske*.

The filter contents were developed by Carl Duisberg, the chairman of the Bayer Leverkusen dyeworks, and Richard Willstätter, 1915 Nobel Laureate for chemistry, with two assistants at the Kaiser Wilhelm Institute. Duisberg produced granules of a light porous mineral, *Diatomit*, soaked in a potash solution which protected against chlorine. To give defence against organic substances and phosgene, the granules were dusted with a fine absorptive charcoal. Professor Haber suggested the Auer Company for the production of the filter container, and an Osram streetlamp screw fitting was used to fix the filter drum to the mask. This 'single layer cartridge' (*Einschichteneinsatz*) was marked '26/8', probably indicating the date in August of its development. By using a removable filter, the Germans were able not only to replace them when they became exhausted, but also to change the contents to counter new gases without scrapping the whole mask. The disadvantage was that the

The French P2 mask with three pads, to protect against chlorine, bromine, phosgene and hydrogen cyanide, as issued from September 1915. The P2 was difficult to adjust and prevented speech. This man has tied a large kerchief around his chin to improve the seal. The rubber goggles are of the type issued in early 1915 to protect French troops against their own tear-gas grenades. (IWM Q61055)

Gendarmes with the 'new model Tambuté' (TN) pad masks, April 1916. This cone-shaped pad mask had a triangular waterproof cover, and was popularly called the *nez de cochon* or 'hog's snout'. The goggles were separate. Carrying bags are worn on the left hip from the belt.

wearer breathed out through the filter, building up carbon dioxide in the face piece. An exhalation valve was considered, but was omitted as too complex for use in the field.

Issue began in September 1915, probably starting in Flanders, then continuing in Champagne during October, and was completed on the Western Front in December 1915 or January 1916. The mask was carried in a canvas bag on the belt, in a cylindrical tin together with two filters in smaller tins.

The French pad masks

The French responded to the problem of German tear-gas with the *Tampon P* (for *polyvalente* or 'general purpose'). Sodium hyposulphite was replaced with a mixture of castor oil and sodium ricinate, which as well as protecting against chlorine and bromine could protect against tear-gas. Thin strips of steel were added to the pad to form a tighter seal around the nose, and it was issued together with goggles. The possibility of phosgene led to the addition in mid-August 1915 of a second pad impregnated with sodium sulphanilate within the same mask, which was then designated the P1. The French themselves adopted the poison gas hydrogen cyanide, which led to the addition of a third pad impregnated with nickel acetate; the three pads were coloured pink, white and green, and the mask was redesignated the P2. In late October the filtration was simplified to two pads by combining the chemicals. Between August 1915 and January 1916 some 4½ million *Tampon P* masks were made.

The *Tampon P* was to be severely tested when the German Pioneer Regt 35 returned to the West in the autumn, when cooler conditions were more suitable for cloud attacks. A series of cloud attacks around Reims began on 19 October on a 7½-mile front. German sources state that they dug in about 14,000 cylinders and used phosgene for the first time, mixed with chlorine on a ratio of 1:4. Doctor Kling went to investigate the day after this attack, but as he made his way along a communication trench just in front of Fort de la Pompelle a heavy bombardment began, followed by the whistle of gas being released from cylinders. Unable to use a gas sampling bulb, he deliberately inhaled some gas in order to identify it, and detected only chlorine. Kling learned for himself how difficult it was to adjust the *Tampon P2* in an actual attack, and that its effectiveness was relative.

The gas attack lasted for half an hour, with intervals of smoke, after which the German infantry attacked. They took some trenches abandoned in panic by a Territorial regiment, but were forced to withdraw when they found them still full of gas. The French casualties from the attacks of 19 and 20 October were extremely high: 750 killed and 4,200 evacuated, more than half of the latter seriously injured. The high casualties suggested phosgene, but Kling found no evidence of it. Even with this first-hand experience, Kling and other scientists concluded that the masks were not being used properly and that, when they were, there was almost no poisoning.

The Germans attacked again on 27 October, releasing a huge quantity of gas; civilians 7½ miles from the front were affected, the sky was darkened by the clouds, and chlorine was smelt in Châlons, 18½ miles away. The attack was solely intended to cause casualties and demoralize the French, and German infantry made no attempt to follow it forward. A further German chlorine cloud attack north-west of Verdun on 26 November once again revealed the weaknesses of the P2 mask, and also the need for better French anti-gas training (see Plate C). A large number of men were also affected by *Palite* shells, against which the P2 mask gave no protection.

The French had already resolved to replace the *Tampon P* as soon as possible. It did not protect against high concentrations or attacks of long duration, and the chemicals were quickly exhausted because only that part of the pad directly in front of the mouth was breathed through. Kling was anxious to provide protection against *Palite* as well as other tear-gases. A team under Paul Lebeau, Professor of Toxicology at the École Supérieure de Pharmacie de Paris and a leading member of the committee for French gas protection, wore masks while exposed to the various gases until the effects were impossible to bear. They tested three new designs of mask in October, in more rigorous trials that including running and speaking while wearing them.

One model, the design of Sgt Auguste Tambuté, an outfitter responsible for the manufacture of masks, was superior. It consisted of a cone-shaped pad enclosing the nose and mouth, and had the advantage of taking the impregnated pad out of contact with the mouth, allowing the user to speak. Like the P2, it was worn with separate rubber goggles, and used three differently impregnated pads; but it formed a better seal around the face and chin, and allowed more of the pad's surface to come into play for neutralizing the gas. On 3 November, Prof Lebeau recommended the modification of the mask with an elastic strap passing over the top of the head and, like the *Tampon P*, a metal strip moulded to the shape of the nose. The first 2,000 of these *Tampons T* (for Tambuté) were sent to the Fifth Army on 17 November 1915.

While investigating the 26 November attack a medical chemist, Dr Charles Flandin, found evidence of something more disturbing than *Palite*. In a bombardment of about 300 gas shells near Avocourt the usual symptoms of throat or eye irritation had not been reported. Soldiers removed their masks without apparent ill effects, but then experienced an increasing sense of giddiness and constriction of the chest. After two

or three hours their condition had become serious: five died and 75 or 80 were evacuated during the night, of whom another six died over the next few days. The lack of lachrymatory symptoms and the delayed action suggested to Flandin the use of phosgene rather than *Palite*, as did the cause of death revealed by post mortem examinations. There was no lingering smell in the shelled area, which was not surprising, but on a piece of one of the shells Flandin believed that he detected the odour of phosgene. Doctor Kling was sceptical, and searched without success for actual traces of phosgene in used respirators, in shellholes and in the internal organs of the dead men.

There were growing signs that if it had not been used already, then phosgene was about to be employed by the Germans in the near future. In response to the attack of 26 November the French government authorized on 18 December the manufacture of phosgene, and it became ever more imperative that the French mask should protect against this gas. Initially the number of pads in the *Tampon T* was reinstated to two, one of castor oil and sodium ricinate and one of *Néociane*, which was more effective against phosgene; it was also found to protect against chlorine for half an hour. Work was begun to improve the T mask to make it faster to put on, and a waterproof cover was added. The resulting mask was known as the 'new model Tambuté' (MTN or TN), the first examples of which where produced in January 1916.

By February an estimated 3.5 million T and TN masks had been sent to the front; production reached 6.8 million for the TN and one million for the T model. Owing to the increased use of gas shells and the complexity of adjusting separate mouthpiece and goggles, two versions were made with integral goggles or eyepieces, known as the TNH and LTN.

Phosgene attacks, and the British PH Helmet

The first substantiated phosgene attack fell upon the British. At the end of October a second German gas unit, Pioneer Regt 36, moved to the Ypres sector. After installing cylinders around Hooge they found that the wind was wrong, and they moved them to a 3-mile-wide front stretching from the Ypres Canal to south of Wieltje. The British expected phosgene to be used, and raided repeatedly to obtain a prisoner with information. An Unteroffizier was captured, and questioned by an intelligence officer and Leslie Barley, now Chemical Adviser to the Second Army. When he refused to talk they locked him handcuffed overnight in the freezing roof space of the town hall in Cassel; and at 5am the next morning he duly revealed the time and location of the attack.

On 19 December 1915, shortly after 5.15am, the Germans opened 9,300 cylinders, probably containing 177 tons of chlorine and phosgene at a ratio of 4 to 1. Attacking at night meant that there was a greater chance of surprise, and that the ground was cooler and the gas less likely to rise. The gas passed over in about half an hour. All the troops had by this time been issued with P Helmets and, although some were reported to have fallen to pieces when put on, the remainder provided sufficient protection. The Germans followed the cloud gas at about 6.15am with a heavy gas shell bombardment; these exploded with a dull splash, and affected some men before they realized what was happening. There were other signs of inadequate gas-training (a lance-corporal in the 6th Duke of Wellington's shot himself after being gassed); but once the gas had passed over, members of the 1st King's Shropshire Light Infantry starting singing, taunting the Germans to attack. The Germans had intended to send 20 patrols over, but only two could get forward. The number of British gassed was 1,069, of whom 120 died; although this reflected the deadly nature of phosgene, the figures were lower than the French losses in October.

Barley definitely identified phosgene, and a simple test was the 'tobacco reaction', when smokers discovered that the presence of phosgene left a peculiar taste. Phosgene is over ten times more toxic than chlorine. Although smelling of musty hay, it could be difficult to detect in small but lethal concentrations and, unlike chlorine, it did not cause a spasm on inhalation. It could also have a delayed action, and victims might be apparently unaffected for hours before death.

Although the British helmets had severe limitations, work proceeded on the principle of adding chemicals to the fabric. The P Helmet had a strong chemical smell, especially when exposed to chlorine; it had poor visibility, and was vulnerable to rain. The caustic phenate could cause severe blistering on the forehead or neck, especially after rain or in hot weather, when the helmet caused profuse sweating. Above all, it only protected against one part phosgene in 10,000, and would fail if the Germans could achieve a higher concentration.

In mid-September 1915 a report was received from Russia of an effective absorbent of phosgene called hexamine. However, the staff at Millbank could find no way of incorporating it into the P Helmet. The problem was solved at the end of October by Capt Samuel Auld, former Professor of Agricultural Chemistry at Reading University, who ran a facility behind the British lines at Abbeville for re-dipping P Helmets.

From 20 January 1916, all helmets were dipped with the phenate-hexamine solution and were designated the PH Helmet. By July 1916 virtually all British troops had received this helmet.

The Phenate-Hexamine Goggle (PHG) Helmet, a variant of the PH, incorporated sponge-rubber tear-gas goggles and elastic around the head. It was introduced on 13 January 1916 to protect artillerymen from tear-gas shells, and issued initially at 24 per battery (see Plate D).

The British Large Box Respirator

The impregnated cloth of the PH Helmet could still stop only a limited amount of gas, and if the Germans could liberate high concentrations of phosgene, the helmet would fail. There was also every reason to expect that the Germans would use new gases against which it would be impossible to adapt the PH. In early August 1915, Bertram Lambert, a lecturer in chemistry at Oxford University, developed lime and sodium permanganate granules which dealt effectively with a range of gases. His idea of using the granules in a layered filter inside a box was taken up at Millbank. The German 1915 respirator, which was under development at the same time, relied in part on charcoal, but it was impossible for the British to produce charcoal of sufficient quality. Only bone charcoal was available in quantity, used for decolourizing sugar, but this was not as effective as the German charcoal.

Lambert worked with Edward Harrison and John Sadd at Millbank to devise a method of mass production of the granules. Harrison, an experienced research chemist, emerged as a key figure in the design of a suitable respirator, known during development as 'Lambert's' or 'Harrison's tower'. The basic model actually used the British Army water bottle as a 'box'; in its later form the filter contained three layers comprising lime-permanganate granules, fragments of pumice soaked in sodium sulphate solution, and fragments of bone charcoal. The box was carried in a satchel slung over the shoulder, and was connected to the mouth by a corrugated rubber tube. Sadd designed a metal mouthpiece, held in the teeth, and a facemask of multi-layered fabric that was held on the head by elasticated tapes; it also contained a nose clip. The fabric was soaked in a zinc-hexamine solution developed by Harrison. Attached to the

The 'Respiratory Tower' or Large Box Respirator was intended for machine-gunners, artillerymen and Special Brigade personnel, but is worn here by an Australian chaplain, almost certainly the renowned Maj Walter Dexter, DSO, DCM, in the Bois Grenier sector on 5 June 1916. It was worn with the 'Rubber Sponge Goggles', which were also issued separately as tear-gas protection. (IWM Q670)

underside of the mouthpiece was a rubber exhalation valve. The mask was worn with a separate pair of sponge-rubber goggles.

The resulting device, called the 'Large Box Respirator', was a complex apparatus, the manufacture of which was entrusted to Boots of Nottingham. It was considered too bulky for use by the infantry, and the earliest issue was to the Special Companies themselves in the winter of 1915/16. In mid-February 1916, 7,500 examples of the 'Respiratory Towers' were sent to each of the three BEF armies on the Western Front for issue to machine gun and artillery personnel, and up to June 1916 about 200,000 were distributed (see Plate D).

There was undoubtedly frustration amongst the scientists at the retention of the fabric helmet, and the limited issue of the Large Box Respirator was regarded as a subterfuge to persuade the authorities that it should be issued universally. The three key breakthroughs of British gas defence had all occurred independently of the Royal Army Medical College at Millbank: this, and the discovery of faulty testing of P Helmets, was probably what led to the dismissal of Lelean as head of the college at the end of 1915.

GAS WARFARE DEVELOPMENTS, 1916

German attacks, 1916

For both sides, cloud gas attacks were now seen as part of the war of material and attrition, rather than of breakthrough; essentially, they aimed simply to cause casualties and lower morale. Only small-scale attacks or raids were attempted following gas clouds. The Germans launched about 20 cylinder attacks during 1916, using at first a ratio of 80/20 chlorine to phosgene, and later 50/50.

They altered their tactics to deal with opponents equipped with improved respirators, discharging the gas as rapidly as possible in such a dense volume that one breath would cause immediate choking, preventing the surprised victims from getting their masks on. All attacks were made at night or early morning, when the gas was less likely to rise over the cool ground and when it was harder to detect. They chose quiet sectors, switching between fronts, but the preparations meant that the Allies were often forewarned. Fast release meant that the attacks lasted for a shorter time, sometimes only ten minutes. Once men's masks were adjusted there was less chance of the gas doing harm; but by creating a highly dense cloud and increasing the proportion of phosgene, the Germans attempted to exhaust the respirators.

They also tried subterfuge. At Hulluch on 27 April, although the British were warned of gas by a deserter and an exodus of rats, the Germans surprised them by first releasing smoke followed an hour and a half later by gas. After the smoke attack men discarded their PH Helmets, and thus suffered heavy casualties in the actual gas attack. There were high casualties on occasions when training and gas discipline was poorer, including men mistakenly removing their helmets due to irritation caused by the strong smell or stuffiness and succumbing to gas, as had occurred at Loos. In many cases the Germans succeeded in penetrating the Allied respirators, and the limitations of the British PH Helmet were clearly shown.

The casualties were worst where trenches were close together, because men had less time to get their helmets on and the density was highest. After an attack of 29 April at the Kink, a trench just 50 yards from the Germans, almost every man was found dead from gas, each with his helmet properly fitted. After the same attack, all the dead in 16th Division were also found wearing their PH Helmets. Casualties were blamed officially on bad gas discipline and a batch of helmets not having been properly impregnated; in reality, the PH Helmet could not keep out a sufficient concentration of phosgene. Its failure now clearly demonstrated the urgent need for the Small Box Respirator then under development (see below). In the last of the attacks against the British, at Ypres on 8 August 1916, a relief between units was taking place, many soldiers were inexperienced, and the crowded trenches made it harder to get helmets on. The gas was so concentrated that helmets had to be worn at Poperinghe, 8½ miles behind the front line. British casualties from cloud gas in 1916 were 2,796, including 893 killed.

German Gas Pioneers wearing the *Gummimaske* demonstrate the method of cylinder attack, about 1916. The battery, walled in with sandbags, appears to contain 14 cylinders; each is fitted with its own rubber hose, which would probably last for one discharge only. The hoses are held in place on the parapet with sandbags. (IWM Q55560)

The Germans suffered a setback in the 29 April attack against Hulluch and the Hohenzollern Redoubt that did much to put cloud attacks out of favour with the German command. Shortly after the discharge of 3,600 cylinders the wind dropped and the gas drifted back over the German lines, causing confusion and panic. The gas personnel of Pioneer Regt 36 could not turn off the valves quickly enough, and had not ordered the evacuation of the front line prior to the attack. Many of the Bavarian infantry had masks in poor or damaged condition, and the concentration was so high that filters broke down; they suffered about 1,500 casualties. The Pioneers themselves had just been issued with the improved *Rahmenmaske*, but had not had time to fit each mask properly, and suffered their own casualties. This disturbance to a quiet sector meant that the attacks were disliked by the infantrymen, and the effects were deemed to be not worth the effort.

The Germans quickly responded to the French use of phosgene shells (see below) with their own lethal gas shells at Verdun, firing them at Douaumont on 9 March and on the night of 4/5 April; they had almost certainly been developing them already. As an agent they chose diphosgene, a less poisonous variant, probably because there was less risk of vaporization or leakage which would disturb the ballistics. Large-scale German manufacture of diphosgene began in April 1916; they called it *Perstoff* or Green Cross according to their colour coding for

French gunners with M2 masks crewing a 90mm M1877 howitzer during 1916. Counter-battery fire was amongst the most effective uses of gas shell. Some of these men have the tin carrying canister for the M2, and some the fabric bag.

gas shells. Initially they tried to create clouds in imitation of cylinder operations, but this required very large numbers of shells; they fired 13,800 near Tavannes on 7 May, and 13,000 at Chattancourt on 19–20 May. At the climax of the battle of Verdun they used 116,000 Green Cross shells on the night of 22/23 June prior to the assault on Thiaumont and Souville, breaking down French Tambuté masks and silencing the artillery. The Germans captured the positions but could not follow up for lack of reserves. Another attempt at Souville, with 63,000 Green Cross shells, was less successful, since the French gunners were protected with M2 masks (see below) and continued firing. The Germans also used Green Cross trench mortar bombs in early 1916, but these were dangerous and unpopular.

During the battle of the Somme the Germans fired Green Cross shells on about 12 occasions in July and nine times in August–September, mainly against the British, causing 2,800 casualties. In October–December, 13 separate gas bombardments caused about 1,300 casualties, this lower figure possibly owing to the introduction of the British Small Box Respirator.

French attacks, 1915–16

French preparations in 1915 for their own cylinder attacks were frustrated by an inability to produce chlorine in quantity; this was also needed to produce and attack with phosgene. They formed *Compagnies Z* of the Engineers, commanded by Cdt Soulié, and recruited slowly from personnel of lower medical categories; it took until November to find 800 men. The first attack, planned for early December in Champagne, was abandoned after installing two-thirds of the cylinders due to the wet ground conditions.

Few senior officers in the French Army were interested in staging gas attacks during 1916, one reason being the danger to their own civilians behind the German lines. The *Compagnies Z* carried out 24 chlorine cloud attacks between February and November. In an attack north of Reims they used 1,300 or 1,400 cylinders, and in another to the east in June fewer than 1,000. In the second half of 1916 they carried out fewer but larger cylinder attacks.

Although it was impossible to obtain the same volume of gas with shells as with cylinder attacks, they had the great advantages of being deliverable to particular targets, achieving surprise, and being far less dependent on wind conditions. French production of 75mm shells was sufficient to allow significant numbers to be diverted to gas; they began using modified shrapnel shells in the second half of 1915. The early shells needed a ceramic or glass lining as the contents attacked the steel. In October 1915, Marshal Joffre, the French commander-in-chief, asked for shells filled with phosgene, which did not require lining. The French mixed phosgene with a smoke-producer to increase the density and assist ranging, but this also reduced the toxicity. Trial shoots on 29 December were disappointing, only 20 per cent of the test animals being killed; but results were better at tests on 19 and 21 February 1916. The French also seem to have fired some shells at the front on the 21st, during the opening of the German assault on Verdun, and these were effective enough for the Germans to report their use.

According to French records, the first use of phosgene shells in action was in March against German positions east of Verdun. This use of lethal gas shells was the beginning of a major new phase in chemical warfare. The French also developed *Vincennite*, based on hydrogen cyanide, which contained an additive to weigh down the lighter-than-air gas, and fired about 30,000 155mm shells at the start of the Somme offensive. Later, the French aimed at silencing German artillery with slow shoots of *Vincennite*. The first, on the Somme at Pressoire on the night of 9–10 October, used 4,000 75mm and 4,400 155mm shells. The same month they shelled the entrance of Fort Douaumont at Verdun with 3,000 155mm shells in two bombardments over 38 hours. After reports from deserters that these bombardments had not been effective, they increased the rate of fire and duration, as well as firing on more precise targets rather than over wide areas. Neither the Germans nor the British regarded *Vincennite* as effective, although the French used it until the end of the war.

A major French chlorine attack during the battle of the Somme, at L'Echelle Sainte Aurin on 12 July 1916. Here the gas is drifting well over the German lines, but during an earlier attack in this sector a wind change sent it drifting back, causing 204 French casualties.

British attacks, 1916

Cylinder attacks were the most common use of chemical weapons by the British in 1916, not least because Col Foulkes favoured this means, but also because of continuing shell shortages. In the autumn of 1915 the decision had been taken to adopt a 50/50 chlorine and phosgene mixture code-named White Star, but it was April 1916 before supplies made this possible, and British cylinder attacks in 1916 were on a smaller scale than those of the Germans. In January 1916, Haig – the BEF commander-in-chief since the previous month – increased the Special Companies to a brigade, with Foulkes in command. By May the Special Brigade numbered around 5,500 men, and included one company each with Stokes mortars and flame-throwers.

Although it was not to have a direct role in the forthcoming Somme offensive, personnel of the Special Brigade RE played a part in the preparatory wearing down of the Germans. During May and June they installed 24,000 cylinders at points along the whole British front. General Rawlinson, whose Fourth Army was to make the assault, initially planned a major attack with 12,000 cylinders on his front, but the weather prevented a synchronized discharge. Instead, 17 separate cylinder attacks were made between 26 and 30 June on the Somme attack front, and 13 against other localities between 27 June and 1 July. No cylinder attacks were made on the Fourth Army front on the day of the attack; but they were used during the battle to keep pressure away from the Somme, and were often accompanied by raids.

An experimental British cylinder release at Puchevillers during August 1916. The four-cylinder manifold used with rubber hoses was invented by Livens, and used by him without authority in the first British attack. It was immediately adopted for all British cylinder operations. The Special Brigade corporals wear the Large Box Respirator. (Higson Papers GS 0759, Liddle Archive, Brotherton Library, University of Leeds)

By the end of November 1916, 110 operations had been carried out using 38,600 cylinders and about 1,160 tons of gas.

The Stokes mortar, first used at Loos, was developed during the battle of the Somme, but was hampered by lack of ammunition. While the gun itself was of simple construction, the bombs for it proved difficult to manufacture. Only smoke rounds were available on 1 July, and were used successfully in places to obscure the advancing infantry from German machine guns. Experienced crews could get 15 bombs into the air at once (see Plate H), but this high rate of fire meant that all 4,300 red phosphorus bombs were used up within minutes, and no support could be given for the rest of the day.

Smoke was also provided for attacks on Guillemont on 16 and 21 August. Even though Col Foulkes had asked for them in July 1915, the first SK tear-gas

bombs did not arrive until September 1916, when the first SK Stokes bombs were fired into Flers and Thiepval on the 24th. As a stopgap, 2in spigot mortar bombs ('toffee apples') were filled with White Star and fired into High Wood on 2 September, as well as at Thiepval and Beaumont Hamel.

Another key British weapon to emerge during the battle of the Somme was the Livens projector. William Livens was a trainee signals officer at Chatham when, believing his wife to have perished on the torpedoed liner *Lusitania*, he vowed to kill an equal number of Germans to the 1,100 passengers and crew who had drowned. He began experimenting with gas- and flame-projectors, and continued even after he had learned that his wife had decided not to sail. He was placed in command of the Brigade's Z (flame-thrower) Company at the beginning of 1916, and his massive fixed flame-projector was used on 1 July on the Somme.

In the days that followed he and another Z Coy officer, Harry Strange, developed a simple mortar for throwing drums of oil. These were buried in rows with only the muzzle projecting, and fired simultaneously by electricity. The British were unwilling to test the weapon at their chemical warfare testing ground at Porton, near Salisbury, deeming it too dangerous; but Z Coy carried out their own trials against the Germans. Twenty burning oil drums were fired on 23 July at Pozières, and more in support of attacks at High Wood on 18 August and 3 September. The principle was also used to throw full gas cylinders at the Germans, resulting in an attack on 28 October, where 135 of these 40lb gas bombs were fired into Y Ravine and Serre, contributing to the capture of these positions two weeks later. Livens referred to his projectors as 'judgements', and after examining the bodies of gassed Germans in the captured positions he claimed that if used on a large scale they could reduce the cost of killing Germans to 16 shillings apiece...

British use of gas shells in 1916 was hampered by a lack of munitions and of the chemicals to fill them, and by the end of the year only 160,000 had been produced. Ten thousand SK tear-gas shells ordered the previous October were delivered by April 1916, but Britain relied heavily on chloropicrin (PS), which was easier to produce. A liquid with a sweetish odour that evaporates quickly at normal temperatures, it would remain in shellholes for about three hours. PS was comparatively effective as both a tear-gas and a lethal gas, but less poisonous than phosgene; however, it had the key advantage that it was capable of

Sgt Martin Fox, C Special Coy, in the Hulluch sector during 1916. Fox's company carried out the largest number of cloud attacks on this front, including an operation of 2,527 cylinders of chlorine-phosgene on the night of 5 October 1916. (REM 6911-03)

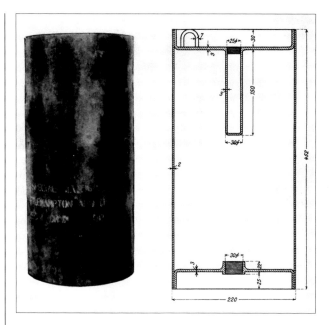

Early drum for the Livens projector, containing White Star (50/50 chlorine-phosgene), as used experimentally on the Somme front in October 1916. (From *Die Feindliche Gasmunition*, January 1918: REM)

penetrating most respirator filters. The Russians used it in August 1915, and the Germans followed, naming it *'Klop'*.

The only other lethal shell available at the beginning of the battle of the Somme contained Jellite, invented by F.A.Brock of the famous firework manufacturers. Brock added chloroform and cellulose acetate to an aqueous solution of hydrogen cyanide, to counter the tendency of this gas to disperse too rapidly. It was therefore similar to the French *Vincennite*, but even less effective.

The seven-day bombardment prior to the Somme offensive required unprecedented numbers of shells. On 16 May, Haig asked for 20,000 gas shells for the 4.5in howitzer, 4,000 for the 4.7in gun, and 16,000 for the 60-pounder, to be supplied by 15 June, plus a weekly supply thereafter. Although these quantities were small, nothing approaching them was available. Of 1,732,873 shells fired during the opening bombardment, only 3,772 were gas (SK). Haig asked on 17 July for all gas shells 'for any nature of gun or howitzer' which could be sent, as he depended for most gas bombardments on the French batteries lent to him, firing *Vincennite* and phosgene. On 31 July he requested 30,000 rounds per week.

The problem of how to dislodge German defenders from trenches, bunkers and cellars was to exercise the BEF throughout the Somme fighting, which lasted until November. In August, the orders were that all gas shells available for the 60-pdr would be needed for counter-battery work, but SK shell could be used against cellars and dug-outs, followed by shrapnel when the occupants were driven into the open. SK was for

SK tear-gas shell for the British 4.5in howitzer. This is the original cast iron shell, as first fired in September 1915. The upper band and the lettering are red, the lower band green. (From *Die Feindliche Gasmunition*, January 1918: REM)

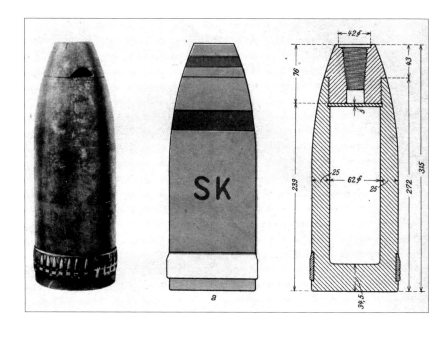

A late (January 1917) *Rahmenmaske*, the improved version of the *Gummimaske* which was shortly to be replaced by the leather mask. The elastic was replaced during 1917 with coiled wire springs encased in cloth. This Austrian-made example has a January 1918-dated 11-C-11 filter; the three layers can be recognized by the parallel raised lines around the filter drum. The container – *Bereitschaftsbüchse* or 'readiness can' – has a short carrying strap.

rendering an area uninhabitable for a long time, Jellite for a rapid effect immediately before an attack, chloropicrin for temporary neutralization to be followed later by an attack, and White Star as the most effective for causing casualties. A concentrated bombardment of SK would render the dug-outs and cellars of a village uninhabitable for at least 12 hours, making it difficult for the British to occupy it themselves. They estimated the number of 4.5in gas shells needed to neutralize a German-fortified village at 4,950 SK, 6,200 chloropicrin, or 7,425 White Star or Jellite. Although more White Star was needed, its combination of casualties and quick dispersion made it more suitable for combining with the assault. The first major use was at the battle of Flers-Courcelette on 13–15 September, when 9,000 shells were fired – a tiny number compared to the 410,000 high explosive shells used in the same operation.

The improved German *Gummimaske*

The Allied use of phosgene and tear-gas caused the Germans to redesign the *Linienmaske* and the single-layer 26/8 filter. Willstätter produced a three-layer filter in November 1915. The outer layer remained unchanged; the middle layer contained conifer charcoal granules to absorb organic substances and phosgene; and the inner *Diatomit* layer was treated with potash and hexamine to break down any phosgene not removed by the charcoal. Issue of this '11/11' filter began at the end of January 1916, and was completed in April. At the same time the fit of the mask was improved, as it was proving difficult for men with lean faces. A framework of fabric was added to the face line to make it more gastight, which gave it the name *Rahmenmaske*, and additional straps were added at the forehead, joining in a Y-shape to pass over the top of the head. Three, later four sizes were introduced, with the number stamped on the front. The diameter of the circular metal plaque into which the filter screwed was reduced from 10cm to 8cm, reducing the volume of air held within the mask and thus its stuffiness.

With the increasing use of phosgene shells by the French the 11/11 filter was judged to be effective, but casualties were suffered because the mask could not be put on quickly enough, there being little or no warning of gas from shells. Units at the front began to manufacture a canister, using in part the tins in which filters were supplied, to form a container in which the mask could be held at the ready and quickly pulled on. In about April 1916 a purpose-made canister was produced, and the respirator was issued with the filter already screwed on. In May the effects of phosgene shelling began to cause exhaustion to German heavy artillery crews forced to wear their masks for long periods. The Germans developed a modified filter to cause less resistance to breathing *(Leichtatmereinsätze)*. These were introduced in June for issue to such crews, and contained larger potassium carbonate granules. In summer 1916 'Green Cross eyepieces' were introduced; coated on the inside to prevent misting, these were only partially successful.

A French medical officer wearing the second pattern M2 mask. The M2 protected for at least five hours against a high concentration of phosgene. However, it was uncomfortable to wear, as both inhalation and exhalation had to be carried out through the pad, and the cone shape trapped air within the mask.

The French M2 Mask

The large number of German gas shells which had both a tear-producing and a lung-irritant effect rendered the Tambuté mask increasingly impractical. Units at the front began to join the goggles and mask together to make it faster to apply, but these failed to give a good enough seal. Small amounts of tear-gas would penetrate the pad, causing serious irritation to the eyes, and GHQ prohibited these improvised models. A series of masks and impregnants were tested during October 1915. When the castor oil-sodium ricinate and *Néociane* pads were adopted for the Tambuté mask in November 1915, it was decided that a design for a full face mask proposed in September by René Louis Gravereaux, a Paris outfitter, should also be introduced.

Gravereaux's design used a broader and thicker pad combined with an eyepiece and a waterproof cover. Like earlier types, the pad formed a pocket which fitted under the chin. On 6 February 1916, 600,000 examples of this 'M2' mask were ordered, and it was introduced in March. The eyepiece was made of hydrocellulose, or cellophane, supposedly to absorb the moisture that would cause it to mist up. The mask could be put on very quickly and was kept in place by elastic and cotton tapes. Initially only one size was made; men with abnormally sized heads continued to wear the TN and goggles. It was issued at first in the same metal container, but had to be folded to fit, which caused damage to the eyepiece.

As a result, a second model M2 with two circular eyepieces was introduced in April 1916. At first these were double-layered, the outer being glass, the inner cellophane. However, the difficulty of wiping the inner eyepiece, which became misted after a half-hour's wear, led to replacement with single-layer thicker cellophane or cellulose acetate eyepieces with a demisting coating. The second model came in three sizes. Between May and November 1916, 6.2 million M2 masks were issued; the delay in producing an improved model meant that it was worn throughout 1917 and was in use until August 1918.

The British Small Box Respirator

The success of the Large Box Respirator led to the universal issue of a more compact version. Edward Harrison, John Sadd and the other Millbank staff developed the Small Box Respirator, which could be carried by an infantry soldier without undue encumbrance. They reduced the filter in size by placing lime-permanganate granules between two layers of bone charcoal, which kept out both lung irritants such as phosgene and the heavy lachrymatory vapours. The mouthpiece was connected to the corrugated rubber tube by a brass right-angled junction, which also contained an exhalation valve. Saliva was prevented from running down the tube into the filter box by a flange which drained it into the exhalation valve. Like the German mask, the facepiece

The inlet valve of the filter box of a 1916-dated Small Box Respirator, consisting of a rubber disc held by a stud in the centre of a perforated metal plate. The sides of the box were corrugated to ensure that the gas passed evenly through the filter materials. Boxes were painted black until the introduction of the NC filter in July 1917. (Steve Chambers)

was made in four sizes, the number being stamped on the front. A prototype was ready in May 1916, and examples were sent to France for comparison with the German respirator. The first order for 100,000 was placed on 16 June 1916, and was soon raised to half a million. Every soldier was individually fitted with his mask, and then exposed to tear-gas in a chamber for five minutes.

Second Army at Ypres was equipped first, from the end of August to 19 September; issue to First Army was completed in late October, followed by the other armies. All Large Box Respirators and PHG Helmets were withdrawn, and each man now carried a Small Box Respirator and a PH Helmet as a back-up; the latter was finally withdrawn from front-line troops in February 1918. Edward Harrison, providing both research and organizational genius, took over the Anti-Gas Department at the end of 1916.

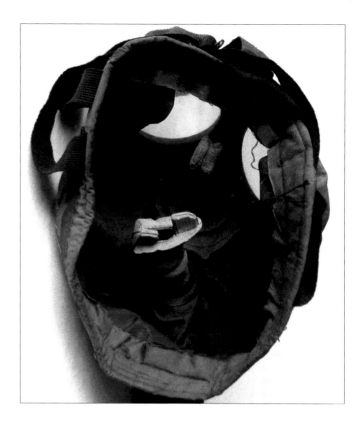

Interior of the facepiece of a British Small Box Respirator. The rubber mouthpiece was held in the teeth, and used with a nose clip to prevent accidental inhalation. The wearer was additionally protected by a rubberized impermeable facepiece copied from the German mask, which provided eye protection and incorporated folds to allow wiping of the inside of the eyepieces without removing the mask.

GAS WARFARE DEVELOPMENTS, 1917

German attacks

The Germans responded to improvements in Allied protection with fewer cylinder attacks in 1917. They carried out no more against the now well-protected British, but staged large-scale chloropicrin attacks against the French in an effort to penetrate the M2, which now offered improved phosgene protection. On the afternoon of 31 January, east of Reims, they emptied 18,600 cylinders on a 7-mile front, causing 531 deaths and 1,500 injuries. Attacks near the coast in April and June killed 470 and 367, and two in the quiet sector of Lorraine in April and July killed in the region of 130 men in each attack. The second was the last cylinder attack by the Germans on the Western Front; one prepared in August in Champagne was abandoned when the French artillery destroyed the cylinder emplacements.

In September, in an unusual attack, the Germans attempted to flood part of the Béthune coal mines with almost 8 tons of chlorine-chloropicrin. French miners still worked this system even though one shaft, well over half a mile deep, ran behind the German lines. British tunnellers entering the system to rescue French coalminers and their own personnel were compelled to turn back after almost a mile when the face masks of their Small Box Respirators were penetrated. A relief party, their masks sealed to their faces with tape, were also forced back. The bodies of some miners were eventually recovered after LtCol Logan RAMC

(continued on page 41)

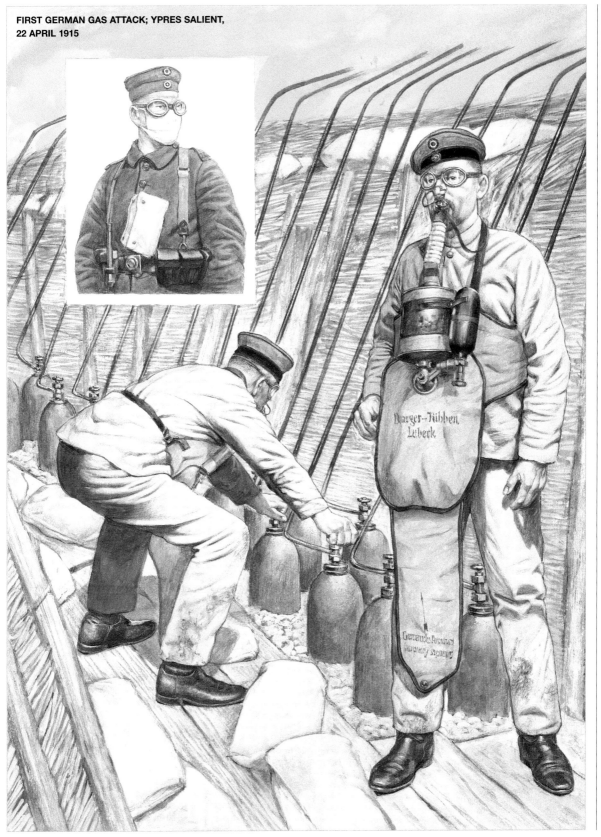

A

B

BRITISH GAS ATTACK: BATTLE OF LOOS,
25 SEPTEMBER 1915

GERMAN CLOUD ATTACK ON FRENCH TRENCHES;
BÉTHINCOURT, 26 NOVEMBER 1915

C

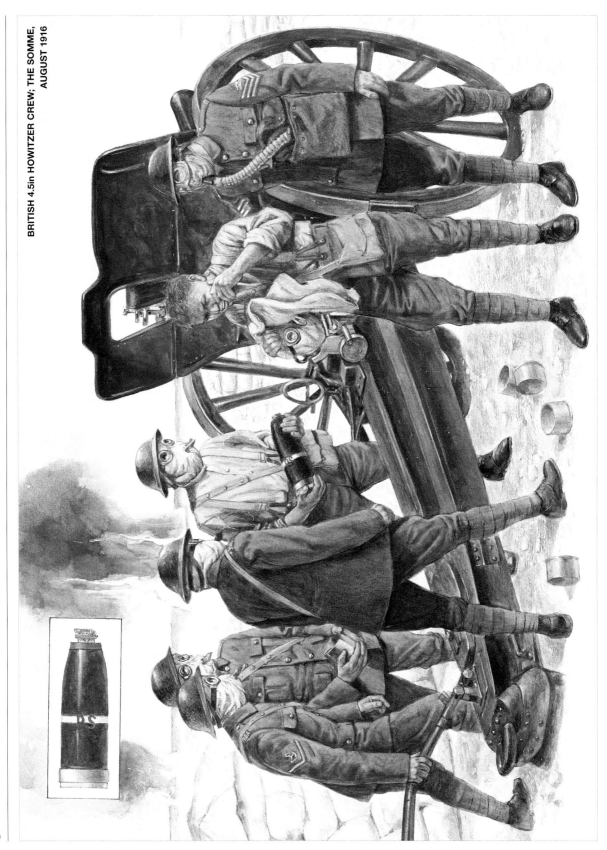

D

BRITISH GAS ALARM POST; GIVENCHY,
FEBRUARY 1918

E

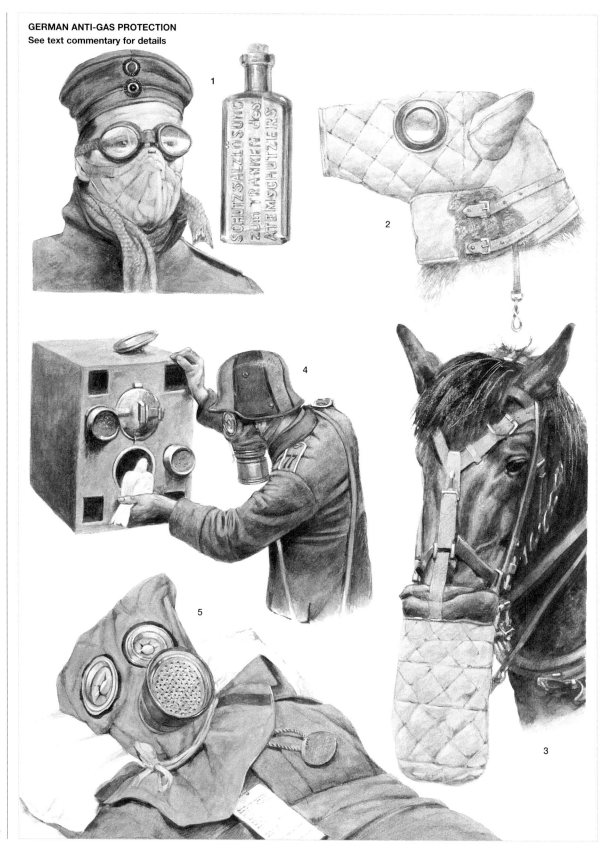

F

G

US ARMY STOKES MORTAR CREW; ST MIHIEL, 12 SEPTEMBER 1918

H

improvised respirators from a German face-piece and two British filter boxes. The German Gas Pioneers continued some harassing cloud attacks on the Russian Front until November, when that front disintegrated.

German gas shell instructions of February 1917 specified the most favourable atmospheric conditions, including a wind speed not exceeding 3½mph, and the need to feed the target with gas by slow fire over a period of hours. In particular the instructions emphasized the need for a large number of shells to be used – a combination of 21,000 light, medium and heavy shells for roughly each square half-mile of an area shoot, or the equivalent to 41 tons of Green Cross. This was less than would be achieved in a cloud attack, but enough to make the targets wear their masks for long periods.

In searching for lung irritants of greater persistency, at the beginning of 1917 the Germans Dr Lommel and Prof Steinkopf proposed a substance previously rejected as insufficiently toxic. Their names gave it the designation '*Lost*', although it was also called by the Germans Yellow Cross and by the French *Yperite*. To the British and Americans it was mustard gas; and it was to be the most effective of all warfare gases.

A dark oily liquid with a very low boiling point, and a faint smell of mustard or garlic, it was known to cause blistering and conjunctivitis, but these symptoms were initially not thought to be significant tactically. The Germans fired 50,000 mustard gas shells east of Ypres on the night of 12/13 July 1917, and were astonished when they learnt from prisoners that they had caused thousands of casualties – not through lung irritation, but by blistering of the skin and blindness. The Germans introduced another new agent in July 1917, diphenylchloroarsine (DA), which they classified as Blue Cross. As a fine dust this could penetrate a respirator and cause intense pain to the sinuses, forcing soldiers to remove their gas masks and succumb to phosgene shells fired simultaneously. This was the theory; in fact the detonation failed to create small enough particles, and only rarely did Blue Cross shells have a serious effect on Allied troops. Lack of field trials meant that the Germans did not grasp how unsuccessful the method was, and wasted production on ten million Blue Cross shells in 1917–18.

For the remainder of 1917 the Germans used fewer mustard and Blue Cross shells, partly because of difficulties but also because reports of the persistency and blistering effects led them to revise their gas tactics. They tried out new methods in the late summer campaigns in Russia, where their use was less likely to alert the French and British. They also doubled the capacity of gas shells by introducing longer shells with thinner walls. In late 1917, however, they increased the high explosive content, which disguised the tell-tale 'plop' sound but reduced the amount of gas and scattered it more thinly.

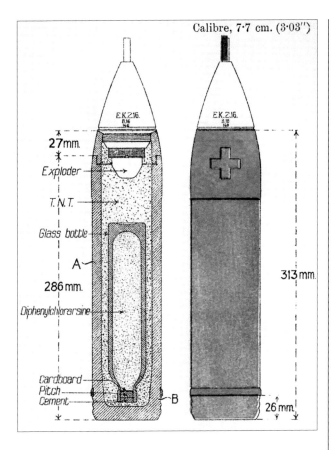

German 7.7cm field gun Blue Cross shell with the EKZ 16 instantaneous impact fuse. The Germans attempted to disperse DA (diphenylchlorarsine) by filling glass bottles with the solid and embedding them in the explosive, but it did not create fine enough particles to penetrate Allied respirator filters. The shell was painted yellow and blue with a blue cross on the upper yellow portion. (From *Notes on German Shells*, May 1918: REM)

British attacks

During 1917 the Special Brigade refined cylinder attacks in both technique and the gases used. White Star (chlorine and phosgene) continued to be the standard filling, but chloropicrin was tried, mixed with hydrogen sulphide (making Green Star), or chlorine (Yellow Star), to penetrate German masks. In the La Bassée-Loos–Hulluch sector, personnel of C Special Coy staged a series of large-scale discharges with a variety of agents used repeatedly against the same sectors.

On 1 September 1917 they used White Star, Red Star (pure chlorine) and Yellow Star in a 1,334-cylinder attack at Hulluch. A month later they gassed the same trenches, while neighbouring sectors were bombarded with phosgene and chloropicrin from Livens projectors and Stokes mortars. Gas was used continually to harass, exhaust, injure and kill troops away from the main fighting fronts, so that there was no quiet sector for the Germans to rest. By attacking in the French sector at Dixmuide the British caught the Germans by surprise with a 1,000-cylinder attack on 26 October. Concentrated chloropicrin could equally penetrate the British respirator, as on 5–6 November, when a wind change killed one and severely injured 11 of C Company. From 16 June 1916 to 4 April 1917 Special Brigade discharged 42,600 cylinders, equal to 1,145 tons of gas; from April to November 1917 it used just 12,000 cylinders, or 328 tons of gas.

Improvements were made to the Stokes mortar: a fuse lit while the bomb rested at the top of the barrel was replaced with a sprung lever. A more plentiful supply of ammunition allowed Special Brigade to

The Livens projector. These tubes were dug into the ground at an angle of 45 degrees, and the range was altered by the size of charge. Three lengths of tube were tried, but the most common was 36 inches. The projectiles were 7.6in diameter drums, which were filled with phosgene at Calais. (From Foulkes, 'Gas!'...)

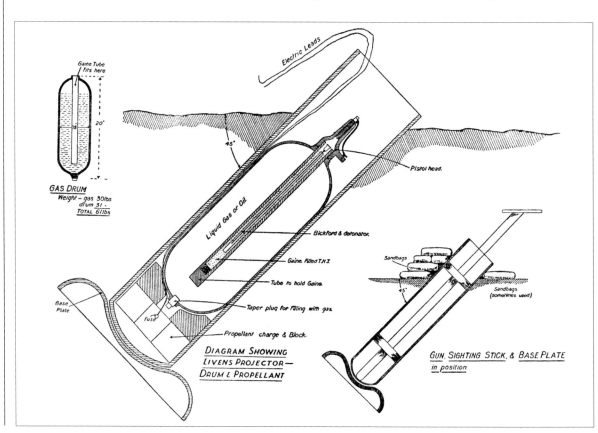

GAS DRUM
Weight – gas 30lbs
drum 31 .
TOTAL 61lbs

DIAGRAM SHOWING LIVENS PROJECTOR— DRUM & PROPELLANT

GUN, SIGHTING STICK, & BASE PLATE
in position

fire about 100,000 Stokes bombs in 1917. Phosgene and chloropicrin were used in combination to force Germans to remove masks. White phosphorous rounds were available as both an effective smoke bomb and an incendiary. Thermite bombs, containing powdered aluminium and iron oxide burning at 3000° C, were timed to burst in the air to force soldiers out of dug-outs, and to set fire to woods, emplacements and men. They were fired accompanied by smoke on to German positions as the British infantry were crossing No Man's Land at the battles of Arras and Messines.

Gas would be used during the days leading to an attack. A fortnight before the battle of Messines, 1,000 chloropicrin and 992 SK bombs were fired at the River Lys positions – the chloropicrin to inflict casualties, and the SK to cause prolonged wearing of the respirator, preventing repair work to damage caused by the artillery. These were followed several hours later by 100 rounds of thermite to cause further confusion. Stokes mortars were also combined with Livens projectors. Gas was not used where it could affect the attackers, but 295 SK, 188 phosgene and 190 chloropicrin rounds were directed at German counter-attack troops. SK was found to be too persistent for the short range of the mortar, and no more was requested after May, although stocks were used up. The use of mixes of Stokes bombs in combination was common from mid-1917. For an attack at Monchy on 1 December 1917, thermite was used to drive Germans out of dug-outs, followed by phosgene, then chloropicrin to force them to remove their masks, and finally more phosgene. The attack involved 44 mortars firing 2,300 bombs and lasted just 15 minutes.

The Livens projector became a formidable weapon in 1917, capable of overcoming German masks by surprise and concentration of gas. In December 1916, GHQ ordered 15,000 projectors and 50,000 projectiles; and by the Armistice, 140,000 projectors and 400,000 projectiles had been supplied. Usually they were fired at night, disrupting ration parties and causing misery and usually casualties amongst soldiers in the front lines. These tactics contributed to the Germans thinning out their front-line positions during 1917 and 1918, and adopting defence in depth. Accuracy was not the intention of the projector, as several hundred would be fired simultaneously at areas rather than precise targets. Firing was by electricity, with a huge flash and explosion and a cloud of white smoke from the powder propellant.

General Allenby was persuaded to use the Livens projector following a demonstration when a bomb hit its target by fluke. The attack by his Third Army at the battle of Arras was the debut of the projector on a grand scale, convincing GHQ of its worth and creating alarm in the German command. An attack was made five days before the assault to disorganize the German defences; and Special Brigade fired 2,340 projectors from 31 locations at 6.15am on 4 April, launching 50 tons of phosgene and chlorine on to German trenches, gun positions and command posts. From April to November 1917, 97,000 drums were fired in 25 attacks, mostly to support raids or harass rear areas. The largest single operation of the war was four days before the battle of Messines, when 1,500 drums of flammable oil were fired into German positions in conjunction with Stokes mortar attacks. They were also used during July prior to the opening of the Third Battle of Ypres; and in a large attack prior to the tank attack at Cambrai, 4,200 were fired into Bourlon Wood on the night of 19/20 November. The rapid advance at Cambrai caused the postponement of a very large cylinder, projector and mortar attack.

The British artillery was unable to deliver the concentrations of gas required to penetrate German masks or dug-outs, and instead refined their tactics for neutralization of artillery batteries. In the British offensives of 1917 gas became standard, and the artillery's preferred means of counter-battery work, especially at night when observation was not possible. Less accuracy was required with gas shells, which just needed to fall slightly upwind of the target. A typical counter-battery bombardment opened with 70 lethal shells, followed by SK at 150 rounds per hour mixed with the odd lethal shell. Carried on over hours, this was designed to force German gunners to wear their masks and prevent them firing their guns. This practice used far fewer shells than in 1916; the RA recognized the persistency of SK, and that it was enough to keep the Germans wearing their masks to render them ineffective.

Phosgene shell supply for January–February 1917 was only a third of the 90,000 requested. Haig raised the proportion of gas to other shells to 12 per cent in February, and the demands for gas shells constantly changed as the technology advanced. SK was no longer wanted after March, although it was the only type being produced to target; instead Haig wanted half to be chloropicrin and half phosgene or any lethal agent. In July he again demanded SK, but as a filling for 60-pdr shells for long-range counter-battery work; this in turn was to be superseded by the 6in howitzer. Later in the year pure chloropicrin was replaced by PG (50 per cent phosgene) and NC (20 per cent stannic chloride). SK was replaced by the more effective KSK, which was in turn superseded as a priority by mustard gas after its dramatic effects became known.

Stocks of gas shell steadily increased for the opening bombardments of British offensives, although the earlier battles were fought with the chemical munitions ordered in 1916. In April, there were 40,000 shells for Vimy and 60,000 for Arras; in June, 120,000 for Messines; in July, 154,000 for Third Ypres, and a supply of 34,000 a week. Counter-battery work for the battle of Arras started at 7.30pm the night before the attack with 4.5in howitzers and 60-pdrs, and when the infantry attacked many German batteries were out of action. A German report after Arras acknowledged this, and also the effects of gas on horses, affecting the supply of ammunition to guns. The shortage of effective lethal shells, especially phosgene, meant that direct artillery support for the attacking infantry was less significant.

At Messines gas shell was used during the build-up for harassment and counter-battery fire, and at Zero Hour counter-battery gas bombardments were used again with success. Counter-battery fire for Third Ypres was affected by German use of mustard gas on British artillery positions, but was carried out over three days and nights. German strongpoints were bombarded with 4.5in howitzer gas shells. Again, the German defensive artillery bombardment was ineffective as the British infantry crossed No Man's Land. Artillery and Special Brigade gas attacks preceded each of the attacks of Third Ypres. The British infantry used white phosphorus grenades, and in 1917 phosgene and KSK grenades, although the persistency of KSK left areas uninhabitable for 12 hours. During Third Ypres grenades containing stannic chloride, which could penetrate German filters, were effective for mopping up troops from dug-outs.

German gas projectors, 1917–18

The Germans copied the Livens projector after its use at Arras. The first and most successful attack with the German projector was on the Italian front at the Twelfth Battle of the Isonzo (Caporetto) in October 1917. The Italians had little experience of gas, and poor protection. In September, personnel from Pioneer Regt 36 – wearing Austrian uniforms – reconnoitred positions at Caporetto. At 2am on 24 October they fired 894 projectors, and 5 to 6 tons of phosgene landed in the Italian positions and sank low into the valley, causing heavy casualties. The Austrian artillery also used gas shells to penetrate Italian artillery batteries in tunnelled mountainside emplacements. When Austrian troops (equipped with 4,000 German leather masks) advanced into Italian lines they found 500–600 dead. This victory was more substantial than had been the first use of chlorine at Ypres.

The Germans carried out about 60 projector attacks on the Western Front from December 1917, the bulk of them between April and August 1918. They introduced a rifled version of the projector, with better

Bomb for the German 18cm smooth-bore projector. The Germans used an existing smooth-bore trench mortar bomb for their copy of the Livens projector; it was first used at Caporetto. The three white bands indicate phosgene; the bomb contained 16.5lb of liquid gas. (From *Notes on German Shells,* May 1918: REM)

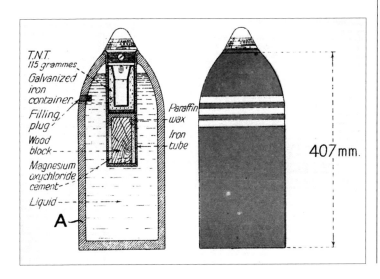

T.N.T. 115 grammes
Galvanized iron container
Filling plug
Wood block
Magnesium oxychloride cement
Liquid
A
Paraffin wax
Iron tube
407mm.

accuracy and range, and added pumice to the filling to prevent the dispersal of the phosgene. However, these refinements missed the point of the effectiveness and simplicity of the Livens projector. They used up to a 1,000 projectors in each attack – this being the equipment of a Gas Pioneer battalion – and they were expected to dig them out after each attack for re-use. The British suffered comparatively few casualties from these attacks, but the French lost more than 586 killed and 1,718 injured by 36 attacks.

German protection: the *Ledermaske*

During 1917 the German mask began to show its limitations. Sudden attacks by Livens projector increased the danger of gas getting caught in the folds of the facepiece. Wearing the mask for more than an hour became extremely uncomfortable; anxiety and heat caused perspiration; and the veins on the head swelled, affecting the gas-tight fit. When rubberized cotton fabric became scarce, a new leather mask *(Ledermaske)* was introduced in August 1917; this used chrome-tanned sheepskin obtained from Bulgaria. The leather was dipped in oil to make it waterproof, and a cone shape cut out, with stitched and lacquered seams designed to make the eyepieces stand proud. The different angling of the eyepieces meant that soldiers had to re-learn rifle shooting in the mask. It was impossible to include wiping folds, which meant that there was less space in the mask where stale air or gas could be trapped. To prevent misting the eyepieces were redesigned, with an outer disc of celluloid and a removable gelatine-coated inner disc. It was also possible

German pioneers laying gas projectors, 1917–18. They spent longer than the British installing their projectors, and waited for the optimum wind conditions, which made them liable to discovery and disruption by artillery. Note the slung metal carrying canisters for the *Gummimaske*. (IWM Q56486)

Bavarian soldiers of Landsturm Infanterie Bataillon Würzburg Nr.1 wait in a dug-out, apparently in readiness to repel an attack in 1917 or 1918. They have the *Rahmenmaske*, with cloth inserted over the filter to protect against chloropicrin and Blue Cross particulates. Note, right, the beard trimmed to allow an air-tight fit for the mask. The same man also has the Dräger oxygen breathing apparatus. Two men in the centre wear body armour. (Mike Hibberd)

for spectacle wearers to insert lenses between the eyepieces. For the straps, elastic was replaced with tightly coiled springs covered with fabric, but it was harder to achieve a gas-tight fit with the leather mask.

The Germans introduced a new '11-C-11' filter drum in June 1917 as a response to British projectors and chloropicrin. The activated charcoal content was increased, and the potassium carbonate reduced. Efforts were made to ease breathing and an apparatus, the *AW–Feldprüfer*, was issued to identify those filters which gave too much resistance.

Allied protection

Recognition that the French M2 mask was reaching the end of its development led Prof Lebeau's team to design a version of the German mask. The result incorporated many advanced features, but took more than a year to develop and manufacture. It was first proposed on 20 April 1916, under the name MCG *(matériel chimique de guerre)* and in August that year 9,000 were made for testing with troops. Professor Lebeau incorporated the system used in the Tissot apparatus (see Plate G2) to prevent the eyepieces misting. The rubberized facepiece of the MCG did not keep out tear-gas, and was replaced with an outer layer of rubber and an inner of fabric coated with linseed oil. An inlet and exhalation valve was incorporated, and Prof Lebeau developed a three-layer filter drum. The mask (see Plate G5) was adopted in January 1917 and renamed the *appareil respiratoire spécial* or ARS. However, mass production did not begin until November 1917, due both to a desire to perfect the design before commencing issue and to problems with raw material supply.

In May 1918, Prof Lebeau devised a new filling for the filter with increased Blue Cross protection. He also developed a fabric filter sleeve impregnated with castor oil to increase protection against Blue Cross and mustard, and these were probably being issued by the time of the Armistice. More than five million ARS masks were produced. The French believed that it was the best mask of the war, although neither the British nor the Germans agreed.

47

In the winter of 1916/17, the British had to modify the Small Box Respirator owing to their use of trench mortar bombs containing the particulate stannic chloride, and fears of the German use of hydrogen cyanide. An extension was devised by Bertram Lambert and H.S.Raper, of cellulose wadding and lime-permanganate granules, which was issued between April and June 1917 to troops in the Ypres Salient. Units had to prise the end off the existing filter box, push the extension over the end and then use sticking plaster to seal it on. This was clearly a far from ideal solution, but the extensions fortunately provided protection against Blue Cross and mustard shells when these were used in July.

A new pattern filter box was designed, which incorporated the wadding and used more efficient wood charcoal and lime-permanganate granules, now mixed together rather than in layers. It was painted brown and was known as the NC filter, after the code for stannic chloride. Respirators with NC filters began to be issued in July 1917 and issue was complete by the end of the year. Also in July, a special version of the Small Box Respirator was introduced for tank crews; this had a separate mouthpiece and goggles, as additional eye protection was needed given the risk they faced from metal fragment 'splash' when under fire.

The first sign of mustard gas in the British lines came on the night of 12/13 July 1917, when a large number of casualties suffering from partial blindness had to be guided to casualty clearing stations. Doctor Claude Douglas, the physiological adviser to the Gas Services, found blisters on their buttocks, genitals and armpits. Within two days many were suffering from bronchitis, and some had died from inflammation of the lungs. By the sixth day the conjunctivitis that caused the blindness had disappeared, but the breathing difficulties were still severe and the blistering had been replaced by skin rashes. The first bombardment injured 15,000 men, of whom between 2 and 3 per cent died over the following fortnight.

British troops temporarily blinded by mustard gas at an Advanced Dressing Station at Béthune, 10 April 1918. The Germans bombarded areas north and south of the Lys attack area on 7–9 April to cut off support from the flanks. Note the soldiers in the background staring at the casualties. (IWM Q11586)

Rapid treatment and secrecy prevented mustard from having a serious effect on British morale. Detection was possible from the smell of garlic or English mustard and, until the Germans modified the shells, from the distinctive 'plop' sound of their bursting. Mustard gas evaporated in sunlight and might not be noticed after a night bombardment until sunrise, when the vapour became dangerous. In winter it could lie dormant for several weeks. Affected men might not know they were contaminated for several hours, felling no pain until conjunctivitis and skin lesions appeared, the sweaty parts being affected worse.

On the night of 20/21 July the Germans shelled Armentières with mustard, injuring about 6,400, including 675 civilians still living on the western outskirts, of whom 86 died. These casualties led to increased issue of M2 masks to civilians still in the zone of the BEF, which included densely populated mining areas, and to the creation of gas-proof rooms. Powdered chloride of lime was the standard means of removing mustard gas, being scattered over the shell craters and surroundings where mustard gas shells had burst. It had to be covered with clean earth, to conceal it from German observation, and because its smell prevented the detection of further mustard gas. It was used as a solution to wash guns, trees, etc that had been splashed. The simplest method to decontaminate clothing was to hang it in the open for four or five days and wash it with bicarbonate of soda.

French measures against mustard gas were aided by their having begun in July to attach a pharmacist, whose duties included anti-gas measures, to each of their battalions. They created decontamination squads in each infantry battalion or artillery battery, although the affected areas were often so extensive that there was seldom enough chloride of lime, and the teams had to choose the key points to treat and prohibit access to others.

From the beginning of August, Prof Lebeau and his team sought an impervious clothing for the squads which could be easily and cheaply produced. The French Ministry of Munitions provided a stock of fatigue overalls impregnated with oil, which were tested at Lebeau's laboratory at the School of Pharmacy, and judged to be adequate on 17 August. The artillery were supplied as a priority. They also arranged production of overalls treated with boiled linseed oil and dyed horizon blue, of impregnated gauntlets and trench boots. Lebeau also designed a haversack made from impregnated fabric to preserve bread rations from mustard contamination.

The British were unimpressed by the French anti-mustard gas clothing, finding that neither the gloves nor the boots – which were ordinary 'gum boots' or Wellingtons – would keep out mustard. Hooded overalls of black oiled cloth were devised in the UK and tested in France. However, the BEF Army Chemical Advisers, in close contact with units at the front, did not consider that the amount of injury suffered from mustard gas warranted special clothing, and concentrated instead on

Member of a French infantry mustard gas decontamination squad, with oil-impregnated overalls, ARS mask, and Vermorel sprayer containing chlorine of lime. His gloves are the type found to be ineffective and replaced by Tambuté's improved model in 1918.

training and discipline. The non-permanent nature of mustard injury led the Chemical Adviser to the Canadian Corps to report in September that he believed men were deliberately exposing their eyes to mustard in order to gain a few weeks rest in hospital.

GAS WARFARE IN 1918

German attacks

In 1918 the Germans used gas shells in unprecedented numbers on the Western Front. Gas was integral to the series of offensives launched in March – the *Kaiserschlacht* – which were their last ditch attempt to defeat the Allies before the arrival of substantial US forces in the front line. They used highly complex artillery tactics developed by Col Bruchmüller, who had tested techniques on the Eastern Front; in September 1917 he mixed Blue Cross and phosgene shells for a bombardment on the Dvina. The Germans developed a complex range of 22 different chemical shells. They simplified the classification to Green, Blue and Yellow Cross: green for lung irritant; blue for sensory irritant, i.e. solids to penetrate respirator filters; and yellow for mustard gas. Green and Blue Cross were non-persistent and were used on troops to be attacked; Yellow was persistent, and would be used against artillery, and to render areas on the flanks and in the rear impassable to seal off the objectives. These complex fire plans were known as *Buntschiessen* ('colour shoots').

For the opening attacks of 21 March against British Third and Fifth Armies ('Michael'), the tactics were successful in silencing the British artillery and caused severe casualties. Against infantry, the mix of phosgene and Blue Cross was 50 per cent of the total shells used; against artillery it was as high as 80 per cent mustard to high explosive. Areas outside the attack zone were heavily shelled with mustard to prevent counter-attacks, such as the Flesquières salient on 10–16 March. Hectare rectangles (2.5 acres) were used to box in batteries with mustard, preventing guns from firing and stopping relief from getting through to the crews.

For the actual infantry attack, the *Feuerwalz* or creeping barrage – long used by the British and French – was adopted, behind which the assault troops followed within 328 yards. Gas in the creeping barrage reduced

Marbache, 8 September 1918: mustard gas necessitated the wider issue of respirators to civilians in the war zones. Most of this family or group of schoolchildren have the new model Tambuté; the girl on the right has the M2, and the woman in the background the ARS. (IWM Q60964)

Hulluch, July 1918: 2nd Lt Martin Fox, C Special Coy RE, with a light rail car loaded for a 'gas beam' attack. This was one of 60 trucks containing in total 1,260 cylinders. The cylinders were opened simultaneously by electrically fired charges. (REM 6911-03)

British resistance, but also hampered the German storm troopers by forcing them to wear gas masks. Supply was complex and different rates of fire were needed for different types of chemical shell. However, mustard was extremely effective as a counter-battery weapon, and British decontamination measures broke down. The March attack was the nearest that the Germans came to fully exploiting the potential of these complex tactics.

In the attacks of 9–25 April in Flanders ('Georgette'), mustard was about one-third of all gas used; Armentières was so heavily bombarded that the gutters ran with the liquid. In the area around Hulluch and Béthune roughly 4,000 civilians were exposed, but precautions already in place meant that only 230 were badly affected and 19 killed. The Germans also used mustard to isolate Mont Kemmel, drenching the north slope while they captured the south. Despite gaining ground the attacks were not decisive.

Gas shells were less effective during the June–July offensives against the French in the south ('Blücher', 'Gneisenau' and 'Marneschutz-Reims'). Attacking in gas masks was especially fatiguing, while Allied casualties were comparatively light. During the 15 July attack at the Marne the wind changed and a gas bombardment killed a significant number of the attackers. The Germans added red and purple aniline dyes to their mustard shells to enable their troops to recognize the contaminated shell craters. This was equally useful to the Allies, of course, who quickly realized that German use of mustard in a locality meant that there would be no attack there for 48 to 72 hours, so they could anticipate German attacks in adjacent sectors. An airburst time fuse was also tried, to disperse the droplets more widely, although it was not used once the Germans were on the defensive.

For the remainder of the year the Germans were in retreat, and mustard gas was to prove far more suited to defence than attack. On 31 July they used 340,000 mustard gas shells to forestall a Franco-American attack west of Verdun. During September–October, British mustard gas casualties were 3,000–4,000 per week, but as the British advance continued German bombardments became less effective and more poorly targeted. It was impossible for the Germans to create their complex fire plans as supply and command became disorganized. When the French advances began the Germans discovered that French troops were less hindered by mustard, having learnt how to minimize casualties when passing through affected areas. Supplies of mustard were less plentiful by September, and the Germans fired off their available shells to slow the American attack at St Mihiel. During October gas ceased to be a factor in halting the Allied advance.

French attacks, 1917–18

French interest in cloud gas also diminished during 1917. Between December 1916 and its last use on 20 March 1918 they carried out 14 attacks, using chlorine-phosgene from the beginning of 1917. It is unlikely that they caused heavy casualties. The French developed the use of gas shells, using the lower concentrations to force German soldiers to wear their masks for long periods. In October 1917 they bombarded German positions for seven and a half hours, causing an entire German division to be withdrawn with exhaustion from continuously wearing their respirators. The French were able to produce mustard gas within a year of the German use, but only by accepting casualties amongst factory workers comparable with those suffered by units at the front. They first used mustard on the nights of 16–17 and 17–18 June 1918, causing 265 German casualties, about 26 of them serious. They found that salvoes fired at intervals were the best way to maintain a concentration around a target over a period of days. In the last week of September 1918 they claimed to have fired as much as 984 tons of mustard.

British attacks

The Special Brigade RE were to become less effective as the Germans thinned out the troops in their front lines in favour of defence on depth, moving the bulk of the defenders out of the range of Stokes mortars and Livens projectors. For this reason, Brig Foulkes (promoted in June 1917) developed long-range 'gas beam' cylinder attacks to send gas deep into the German rear. Cylinders were loaded into rail cars on specially laid track immediately behind the British lines. The gas was released on a narrow front, but was concentrated enough to penetrate German masks deep behind the lines and without warning. A typical attack was carried out on the night of 23 May 1918, when 3,789 cylinders were opened on a 2,000-yard front to send 120 tons of phosgene along the Scarpe valley; it was difficult to assess German casualties.

Nine 'beam' attacks were carried out in 1918, but they did not replace projector attacks. Foulkes used cylinder and projector attacks to keep the Germans in a state of anxiety and to prevent them from resting. In March, 3,000 Livens projectors opposite St Quentin and 2,900 near Quéant served to disrupt the coming German attack. In June, trenches south-west of Arras were hit by 975 drums during a relief, leaving 66 injured and 53 dead. However, the Germans retaliated the following night by shelling the projector site with mustard, causing 126 British troops to be evacuated. The German offensives disrupted plans and led to personnel being taken from Special Brigade, reducing it from 7,000 men in 1917 to 4,500 in March 1918.

When the Allies went on to the offensive from July, opportunities for using projectors and Stokes mortars were limited by the movement of the lines. At Hamel on 4 July, Stokes mortars fired 720 rounds of white phosphorus and 154 rounds of stannic chloride on to the German north flank to prevent observation, and 612 rounds of smoke on the south, to screen the attack without affecting the attackers. After the assault there were two small projector attacks on 6 and 7 July to target preparations for counter-attacks. On the eve of the battle of Amiens of 8 August, Stokes mortars and Livens projectors were used on the left flank two days before, and 175 Livens drums of phosgene were fired into the north flank one day before the attack. There was almost no role for the Special Brigade at the battle of the St Quentin Canal on 29 September, apart from a small projector attack and a smokescreen. By this time the speed of operations was too fast for weapons designed for trench warfare. A method of rapid digging-in of the projector was developed, where it was only buried a foot deep; a wooden sledge mounting a battery of 24 projectors was also towed by a tank. However, by the time targets were located and the equipment brought forward and installed, the Germans had pulled back.

German prisoners wearing 1917 leather masks carry in Canadian wounded during the battle of Amiens, August 1918. (IWM CO2977)

The artillery became more important than the Special Brigade, and 1918 was to see gas established as an integral component of fire plans and with ready supplies of shells. At Hamel on 4 July, gas was used freely in the preparatory harassing bombardment each morning prior to the attack. The 4th Australian Division fired 54 per cent gas shells, and during the night of 23 June its 4.5in howitzers fired 95 per cent gas and 5 per cent smoke. Gas was not fired the night before the attack in order not to impede the infantry moving forward. On the morning of the attack smoke was substituted for gas, in an attempt to make the Germans automatically put on their gas masks and thus handicap their efforts. Tear-gas counter-battery fire with KSK from Zero Hour to Zero plus 150 minutes silenced German batteries in the Cerisy valley. The 4th Australian Division had one of the least difficult advances of the war and – unlike the German *Feuerwalz* – the creeping barrage contained no gas. Once it reached the final objective it switched to gas for counter-battery and to target transport and counter-attack assembly positions, continuing from 10pm to 3.20am the next morning. The counter-battery fire was particularly effective and did most to contribute to the success of the attack. KSK, accurately placed on to pre-located guns, had the power to put a battery out of action immediately, as crews were either blinded or seriously hampered by having to work in masks.

Canadian Army Medical Corps stretcher-bearers wearing the Small Box Respirator somewhere in France in late 1918. This is a reminder that gas shelling forced men to wear protection well behind the front lines. (IWM CO2999)

This process was repeated on a larger scale at Amiens on 8 August, but the advance was to pass beyond the German artillery positions and so KSK was avoided for counter-battery fire for fear of affecting the attackers. Only on the north flank, where a more limited advance was planned, was more used. At Zero Hour, 3.20am, the batteries in the Cerisy valley – which the Germans had not evacuated despite the previous gas shelling – were again silenced with KSK. Thus the German technique of using mustard for area denial was already being followed by the Allies with SK and KSK, especially for counter-battery work. Until August 1918, when it was replaced by mustard, KSK was the main British counter-battery agent. Britain was preparing mustard shells for every calibre of weapon from 18-pdr to 9.2in, for a capability to send mustard to every part of the battlefield.

The battle of Amiens was the peak of British use of gas, as the change to mobile warfare gave less opportunity for its use and presented more danger to civilians in the fighting zone. An exception was the battle of the St Quentin Canal on 29 September, which was also the first use of British mustard gas (as opposed to captured supplies). Mustard was fired throughout the night of 26th on artillery and communication centres, silencing the artillery and causing widespread casualties. The infantry attacked 50 hours afterwards without adverse effects from it. Phosgene, chloropicrin, high explosive and smoke were used for all artillery fire except wire-cutting, with no gas used in the attack path after Zero minus six hours. The shelling at the entrance to the canal tunnel was solely gas, in an attempt to flood it.

One of the casualties caused by a mustard gas bombardment during the British Flanders attack on the night of 13/14 October was Adolf Hitler, then serving with the Bavarian Reserve Regt 16; he was practically blind when he returned to regimental headquarters, his eyes like 'glowing coals'.

German protection

In preparation for their offensives, the Germans issued in March 1918 a clip-on extension to the filter to protect their storm troops as they attacked behind barrages containing Blue Cross shells. Devised by Drs Weigert and Pick at the Kaiser Wilhelm Institute, it contained a special rag paper, but was effective only against low concentrations and caused more resistance to breathing. The Germans changed their filter in May 1918, to increase phosgene protection in response to the Livens projector, with the *Sonntags-Einsatz (S-E)* – so-named because the manufacture dates were changed each Sunday – containing double the charcoal. The S-E filter could withstand a concentration of one part phosgene to 200 of air for 29 minutes.

The Germans made minor changes to the leather mask later in 1918, but the respirator had now reached its limit for development, and instead the emphasis was on gas drill and discipline. The February 1918 edition of the German anti-gas manual instructed improved protection of dug-outs to protect against surprise Livens attacks. During 1918, instructions stated that sentries were to be at dug-out entrances at all times and were to check gas blankets and sound the alarm. Working parties were ordered to wear respirators at the alert when within roughly half a mile of the front line.

Allied manufacture of mustard gas caused the Germans surprise and serious concern. Although they had used mustard since July 1917, the symptoms of blistering and blindness were still unknown to their own infantry and gunners. The fastest way to deal with mustard was to re-equip affected men with new uniforms, underwear and boots, but Germany lacked the textile supplies to replace contaminated clothing. This alone placed in question Germany's continuation of the war into 1919. German instructions for the use of chloride of lime as a response to mustard gas appeared on 21 June, and also made specific reference to malingerers who might seek evacuation unnecessarily. In July they formed detection and decontamination squads each of an NCO and six men *(Entgiftungstruppen)* in each battalion. A clothing reserve of 2 per cent was formed, and a limited issue of specially treated uniforms was proposed for the artillery.

An anti-mustard gas ointment, *Gelbolin,* was available in August. By September and October 1918, long gloves and impermeable aprons were being issued to some medical personnel, and ersatz paper fibre overalls for decontamination squads, which were not necessarily impregnated and can have been of little use. Professor Haber himself issued instructions on 27 September, warning against alarmist rumours about the effects of mustard gas; he gave reassurance that the blindness was only temporary, and that mustard did not cause arms and legs to fall off... In October, medical officers were instructed on how to deal with the belief that it caused impotence and genital damage.

Special spectacles – *M-Brillen,* for *Maske* – were manufactured for wear with the German mask, with ear loops instead of metal side frames; these did not affect the air-tight seal around the face. This infantryman, c.1917–18, also carries on his belt a spare filter for his gas mask.

Allied protection

The resurgence of the German use of mustard gas in the build-up to the attacks of spring 1918 exposed the shortcomings of the Allies' protection, and caused casualties to soar.

At the beginning of 1918 the French sought to improve protection against mustard gas because men were suffering serious burns through the gauntlets. In May a hooded jacket and trousers were developed by Tambuté, made of a doubly impregnated oiled fabric. The jacket was joined to the trousers and various fastenings and drawstrings were designed to provide maximum protection. All seams and stitching were sealed with the varnish used on the ARS mask. In July 1918 a gauntlet with a double thickness of fabric was adopted, the two layers being cut so that the weaves were opposing. The French issued an ointment to protect the skin against blistering; this *Pommade Z*, of 10 per cent chloride of lime in Vaseline, was developed by the pharmacists Desgrez, Labat and Guillemard by a process of exposing their own forearms to mustard gas.

Like the French, the British found it impossible to use chloride of lime on the wide areas of ground affected by mustard. In July 1918 it was reported that 1lb or more was needed for each 7.7cm shell crater. Treated shellholes would be clear in anything between two hours and two days depending on weather conditions, but if untreated could be dangerous for three weeks or more. A heap of chloride of lime was to be left at dug-out entrances, and men ordered to walk through it before entering. Blistering could be prevented if the affected skin was rubbed immediately with dry chloride of lime, but it was often impossible for the victim to know if he was affected until it was too late. As the Allies began to advance in August, they could not maintain the stocks of chloride of lime and fresh uniforms needed to counter the lavish German use of mustard gas to cover their retreat.

US signallers serving with the AEF repair wire, wearing the Small Box Respirator. The Americans manufactured the SBR in 1917, but the first issue failed under testing. They produced an improved version, the Corrected English Mask, from October 1917; 1.8 million of these were manufactured. In February 1918 the Richardson, Flory & Kops (RFK) mask was introduced, of which 3 million were made before the Armistice. Both were externally similar to the SBR but can be distinguished by the metal guard for the exhalation valve. (IWM Q60987)

Lt Donald Grantham with 'M Bombs', the first air-dropped chemical weapons; Lake Onega, North Russia, September 1919. The thermogenerator was a large hand-thrown grenade which produced a highly irritating arsenic smoke. It was designed to be thrown downwind by trained infantry at 15,000 per 20,000 per mile of front, as a prelude to an attack. When Maj Thomas Davies arrived at Archangel with 50,000 thermogenerator, he found the country too densely wooded for any chemical weapons that relied on the wind. He adapted them for use as aerial bombs by adding fins and a padded nose cap, and they were dropped on Bolshevik targets by the RAF in small numbers on about ten occasions in August–September 1919. (REM 6911-03)

At the beginning of March 1918, Haig asked for a supply of gauntlets for gunners consisting of leather soaked in boiled linseed oil with a cotton outer glove which could be removed and washed. Within a month 42,000 leather gloves and 84,000 cotton overgloves were sent out. As German mustard gas shelling increased later in March overalls were demanded, and some of the black oilcloth suits designed in 1917 were sent out, but were found to be too heavy. In June a lighter cotton drill suit treated with boiled linseed oil began to be issued, and a second design of a knee-length belted coat with trousers. These suits were to be taken off and hung outside before entering dug-outs, and were not to be turned inside out. If heavily contaminated they were to be washed with soap and water, otherwise hanging in the air for several days was sufficient. The problem with the overalls was that it was impossible to have them available when they were needed, except for personnel specially engaged on decontamination. The complexity of their maintenance obviously reduced their utility in actual field conditions, and they were in any case unpopular owing to their discomfort.

Heavy American casualties in autumn 1918 demonstrated the danger of underestimating mustard gas. The AEF produced very thorough measures for tackling mustard, including an impregnated suit capable of resisting it for 60–90 minutes, and portable shower units which could be erected in just 18 minutes to treat and re-clothe 500 men.

From March 1918, the British respirator was fitted with 'triplex' splinterless glass eyepieces in place of celluloid. An officer at Foulkes's headquarters, Henry Sisson, placed a small pinch of DA granules from a Blue Cross shell on to the stove of his room. The smoke produced was so toxic that the whole building had to be immediately evacuated, and no gas mask was proof against it. When the British realized the potential for arsenic smokes to penetrate their respirator they produced another

Clearing a small unprotected dugout

The Ayrton Fan, a canvas flapper, was proposed in May 1915 by Hertha Ayrton, the first woman member of the Institute of Electrical Engineers, as a means of beating back a gas cloud. Although it was tested and rejected several times, Ayrton succeeded through highly placed connections in obtaining its issue by the BEF from April 1916. It was intended as a means of clearing gas from trenches and dug-outs, although fires were more effective in achieving this. Some 104,000 were eventually supplied and, when adopting British anti-gas measures, the Americans ordered 50,000. Ayrton never accepted the worthlessness of her invention, even claiming that it could be used to clear mustard gas vapour. Troops found the handle useful for firewood. (From US gas defence manual, 1918)

extension, in the form of a fabric 'jacket' with layers of cellulose wadding; this was designed in early 1918 and some were issued in early April, but withdrawn in May when the Germans failed to exploit the potential of Blue Cross. In the meantime the box was again redesigned by Harrison and Lambert to incorporate the increased protection. The new design was known initially as the 'XY' respirator, then as the 'Green Band', the filter box being painted black with a central vertical green band. Production began on 9 September 1918, and at the time of the Armistice these were being stockpiled in France ready for issue once the decision had been taken to use the thermogenerator (see below). Along with the thermogenerator, they were sent to North Russia with the expeditionary force in 1919.

Edward Harrison, credited as the genius behind the Small Box Respirator, died of pneumonia on 4 November 1918, the result of overwork and gas inhalation.

Conclusions

By the Armistice of 11 November 1918, Allied gas production had reached that of Germany and was set to exceed it, especially in the USA. The US artillery fired their first mustard gas on 1 November in a bombardment of 36,000 shells north of Verdun. By November 1918, Edgewood Arsenal had the capacity to fill 2.7 million 75mm gas shells per month. They fixed their output of gas at 20 per cent of all shells, to rise to 25 per cent from the start of 1919. By May 1919, US mustard gas production was set to reach 200 tons a day, compared to 18 tons in Germany. Britain planned to treble gas capacity for 1919.

Britain had also perfected the thermogenerator, inspired by Sisson's experiments with Blue Cross filling, which produced an arsenic smoke capable of penetrating all known respirators apart from their own. As well as causing intense pain in the sinuses it also created temporary but extreme feelings of psychological misery. Such was the intensity of these symptoms that human 'guineapigs' at Porton had to be prevented from killing themselves. Brigadier Foulkes was thwarted in his plan to use the thermogenerator on a mass scale in 1919 for a breakthrough attack led by his Special Brigade.

Perhaps a million soldiers were killed or injured by gas during World War I, but it is impossible to determine precise figures. Gas was uniquely suited to the static warfare of the trenches, but once movement was restored there were few opportunities for its use. Under the Treaty of Versailles Germany was forbidden poison gas, and in 1925 the Geneva Protocol prohibited the use of chemical and bacteriological weapons by any power. Their non-use during World War II had more to do with their lack of utility than any moral restraint. Mustard gas was used during the inter-war period in China by Japan, and in Abyssinia by Italy. Iraq used it against Iran and Iraqi Kurds in 1983–88. The common factor was that the victims were unprotected and usually civilians.

* * *

Professor Fritz Haber of the Kaiser Wilhelm Institute, the gifted scientist behind the German chemical warfare programme, received the Nobel Prize for chemistry in 1918 for his pre-war work on the synthesis of ammonia. His covert chemical warfare research after 1918, under the guise of pest control, led to the development of Zyklon B, later used by the Nazis to kill more than a million helpless victims in their extermination camps. Haber, a Jew who had converted to Christianity, fled Germany in 1934 and died shortly afterwards.

SELECT BIBLIOGRAPHY

Many archival records and official publications have been consulted for this survey; the following are the principal published works used:

T.Cook, *No Place to Run* (1999)

C.H.Foulkes, *'Gas!' The Story of the Special Brigade* (1934)

L.F.Haber, *The Poisonous Cloud* (1986)

R.Hanslian & Fr.Bergendorff, *Der Chemische Krieg* (1925)

S.Jones, 'Under a green sea – The British responses to gas warfare' in *The Great War* Vol.1 No.4 & Vol.2 No.1 (1989)

S.Jones, 'The first BEF gas respirators, 1915' in *Military Illustrated* Nos.32 & 33 (1991)

S.Jones, 'The right medicine for the Bolshevist': British air-dropped chemical weapons in north Russia 1919' in *Imperial War Museum Review* No.12 (c.1998)

G.Lachaux & P.Delhomme, *La Guerre des Gaz 1915–1918* (1985)

A.Lejaille, *La Guerre des Gaz* (website) http://pageperso.aol.fr/guerredesgaz/

A.Lejaille, 'La protection française polyvalente contre les gaz de combat' in *Militaria* Nos.226 (2004), 237 & 241 (2005)

O.Lepick, *La Grande Guerre Chimique* (1998)

W.G.MacPherson (ed.), *Medical Services Diseases of the War* Vol. II (1923)

D.Martinetz, *Der Gaskrieg 1914/18* (1996)

Y.Mouchet, 'Les masques à gaz allemands de la Grande Guerre' in *Militaria* No.220 (2003)

A.Palazzo, *Seeking Victory on the Western Front – The British Army and Chemical Warfare in World War I* (2000)

A.M.Prentiss, *Chemicals in War* (1937)

D.Richter, *Chemical Soldiers* (1994)

E.Shepherd, ed. Bruce Rossor, *A Sergeant-Major's War* (1987)

W.Zecha, *'Unter die Masken!' Giftgas auf den Kriegsschauplätzen Österreich-Ungarns im Ersten Weltkrieg* (2000)

PLATE COMMENTARIES

A: FIRST GERMAN GAS ATTACK; YPRES SALIENT, 22 APRIL 1915

Chlorine was discharged at 6pm (German time) by members of Pionierkommando Peterson (nicknamed *'Stinkpioniere')*, wearing Dräger Model 1914 *Selbstretter* oxygen breathing apparatus. Twenty chlorine cylinders were partially buried in the firing step of each emplacement, known as F batteries (for *Flaschen*, cylinder), with lead pipes leading over the parapet. This reconstruction is based on photographs in the history of Reserve Infantry Regiment 239. The exact arrangement of pipes is not known; there may have been a manifold, or individual pipes as here. The *Selbstretter* was an oxygen re-breathing apparatus which used a sodium carbonate cartridge to remove carbon dioxide from exhaled breath and mixed it with oxygen from a steel bottle in a rubberized bag. The Pioneers wear drill fatigue dress *(Drillichanzug)* and *Feldmütze* field caps.

Inset: An infantryman of one of the assaulting units, Res Inf Regt 245, wears the original *Riechpäckchen* respirator. Respirators for the infantry were an afterthought to the gas attack preparations, issued on 15 April. The pads with tapes, made in Ghent, were soaked in a hyposulphite solution and kept in a rubberized bag attached to the front of the uniform. He wears the M1910 field uniform tunic and *Feldmütze*.

B: BRITISH GAS ATTACK; BATTLE OF LOOS, 25 SEPTEMBER 1915

Special Company RE personnel release chlorine while infantry of the Cameron Highlanders wait to attack, 5.50–6.30am. The gas emplacement is based on a sketch by Cpl Richard Gale, Section 7, 186th Special Company RE. Each emplacement contained 12–15 cylinders; on the revetment above is fixed the timetable for the attack and a watch. The RE corporal had to unbolt and re-attach the pipe to each cylinder in turn, and as the gas escaped the valves and joints froze. Another RE corporal uses a Vermorel sprayer with hypo solution to break down the heavy chlorine gathering in the trench; the gas had the effect of turning steel and brass green.

Corporal Gale was in the British front line just north of the Hohenzollern Redoubt, from where the 5th Bn Cameron Highlanders attacked Little Willie trench. Their attack was delayed by ten minutes when the wind failed to blow the gas away from the British trenches. Gale's diary states that some infantrymen were unconcerned by the gas, but others panicked, lifting their P Helmets and inhaling gas. Most wore the helmet rolled on the head in readiness. They are shown in 1914 Pattern leather equipment, with two extra 50-round bandoliers of .303in ammunition; note the vomiting man with two empty sandbags tucked into his belt. The Special Companies wore an armband to identify them and protect them from being ordered over the top; Foulkes chose the colours of the flag of Italy (which had entered the war the day he was appointed). They wore revolver equipment, here the 1914 Pattern.

C: GERMAN CLOUD ATTACK ON FRENCH TRENCHES; BÉTHINCOURT, 26 NOVEMBER 1915

This reconstruction shows an attack at 5.30pm on a trench held by the French 34th Territorial Regiment north-west of Verdun, in the area of Forges and Béthincourt. According to a report by Dr Charles Flandin, who visited the trenches, serious casualties occurred when men were caught in dug-outs eating a meal without their equipment on. Orders were to maintain rapid fire if attacked by gas, but those who were able to use their P2 masks could not see well enough through the mica goggles. The mask was too complicated to put on in a hurry, and let in gas if not tied securely in place. When this happened men tore them off, or attempted to remoisten them with handfuls of snow (centre) or by urinating on them (right). The number gassed in this attack was 387 men, of whom 57 died. The P2 mask and separate goggles were contained in a pouch on the chest.

German pioneers wearing Dräger apparatus practise chlorine discharge at Wahn, 10 February 1915. During a large scale gas release at the Beverloo training ground in Belgium on 2 April, Prof Haber himself narrowly escaped death by gassing when the wind changed. (IWM Haber collection, Q114873)

Cpl Geoffrey Higson RE, D Special Coy, dressed for cylinder gas discharge in March 1916, with a PH Helmet rolled on his head and a valve spanner in his hand. (Higson Papers GS 0759, Liddle Archive, Brotherton Library, University of Leeds)

D: BRITISH 4.5in QF FIELD HOWITZER CREW; THE SOMME, AUGUST 1916

The 4.5in was a very effective field howitzer, and the British weapon mainly used for delivering gas shells in 1916. This battery is being targeted with German tear-gas shells during a counter-bombardment, and these are seen bursting in the left background. All except the sergeant (right) wear the Phenate-Hexamine Goggle (PHG) Helmet, a variant of the PH which incorporated sponge-rubber tear-gas goggles and elastic around the head; this was introduced in January 1916 specifically to protect gunners from tear-gas, and at first 24 helmets were issued per battery. They were suffocating to wear, causing skin sores in hot or wet weather, as seen on the man who has removed his helmet and is also suffering from the effects of tear-gas. The sergeant wears the Large Box Respirator with separate goggles; both this type and the PHG were replaced in late 1916 by the Small Box Respirator.

Inset: 4.5in howitzer shell marked 'PS', indicating chloropicrin, after the Port Sunlight works of Lever Brothers where it was developed. About 8,000 tons were made – although none at Port Sunlight itself, owing to the proximity of housing. The No.44 percussion fuse has a brass safety cap which was removed before loading.

E: BRITISH GAS ALARM POST; GIVENCHY, FEBRUARY 1918

This reconstruction shows a trench held by 1/4th Bn East Lancashire Regt, 42nd Division; the battalion battle badge was a white '4' on a diamond patch. The vane on the parapet (centre) indicates that the wind is blowing from the German lines; consequently the board below it has been turned from 'Wind Safe' to 'Wind Dangerous'. The gas sentry (right) has detected gas and is sounding the alarm; sentries were trained to recognize gas from its smell, and from the sounds of gas hissing from cylinders or bursting gas shells 'plopping'. A large wooden rattle, based on a police type, was introduced in August 1917 to sound a local alarm; when whirled around the handle it made a loud clacking noise. Where cloud gas was detected, the Strombos compressed air horn (right) was also sounded. This was introduced in 1917, replacing the various gongs and bells already in use, although there were in fact no German cloud attacks against the British sectors after its introduction; the rattle was also ordered to be sounded for cloud gas attacks. Dug-out entrances (left) were protected by a blanket kept damped with a hypo solution, using a method worked out by Leslie Barley. The blanket was kept in place on a sloping frame with battens, and when not in use was usually kept rolled up in the wooden shelf at the top. Dug-outs were fitted with two blankets 3ft apart, which were let down when a gas alarm was sounded. All three men have the Small Box Respirator, with its reddish rubber exhalation valve beneath the metal hose connector.

F: GERMAN ANTI-GAS PROTECTION

F1: 1915 *Atemschützer* respirator

Issued August–September 1915, this mask fitted over the mouth and nose, with a metal spring to clip the nose, and was kept in place by tapes tied at the back of the head. It was carried in a small waterproof pouch and issued along with the glass bottle, which contained a hypo solution. The embossed inscription on the bottle translates as 'Protective salt solution for soaking the respirator'.

F2: Dog respirator

The Germans used dogs for messenger and medical services. They were more sensitive to gas than horses, as their noses were closer to the denser gas that lay on the ground. This drawing is based on a British report of August 1918, of an example made of paper fibre and layers of paper gauze impregnated with potassium carbonate and hexamine. The neck portion and earpieces were lined with rabbit fur, and the eye pieces were celluloid.

F3: Horse respirator

Initially the Germans used nosebags filled with damp hay or straw. In 1917 they developed a horse mask, first issued in Italy for the Caporetto offensive. This was made from the same material and impregnation as the dog mask. The eyes were left unprotected. Since horses breathe through the nose only, the seal had only to be around the upper jaw, leaving the bridle free. It was made in three sizes.

RIGHT **British Spicer tear-gas goggles, used from August 1915. An issue of one per man was approved that November and completed for the First and Second Armies in mid-December. The Spicer was less effective than the Rubber Sponge Goggles, which were supplied from March 1916 and were withdrawn in June 1917 when the Small Box Respirator was ordered to be worn for all types of shell gas. (REM RSME0390070)**

BELOW **A Russian demonstration of cloud gas in 1916, with 15 short cylinders linked by individual rubber hoses in an almost exact imitation of the German technique. The Russians made a small number of cloud attacks in late 1916 and early 1917. The officers wear a Russian version of the French *Tampon*, but the watching infantry appear to have no protection. The British and French sent large numbers of masks to the Russians in 1915–16.**

F4: Pigeon box & 1917 leather mask
Various types of carrier-pigeon boxes incorporated respirator filter cartridges. The infantryman wears a 1917 leather mask with the Blue Cross filter extension issued from March 1918.

F5: Head wound mask
Introduced in 1918, this hood-like mask for casualties was made of the same oiled leather as the 1917 *Ledermaske*, with the same filter and eyepieces. The eyepieces were padded on the inside, and a perforated metal cylinder prevented the filter from being blocked.

Germans wearing captured Russian masks. The facepieces are as developed for the Zelinsky-Kumant type in the second half of 1916 (see Plate G1), although the right-hand example is the mask developed by the Russian Mining Institute, which appeared shortly afterwards. In spring 1917 the Avalov mask was introduced, using the same facepiece with a filter incorporating an exhalation valve, but this gave inferior protection. The Russian troops were poorly protected during very intensive gas shelling in the autumn of 1917, when the Germans perfected the methods they were to use in the West in 1918.

G: ALLIED ANTI-GAS PROTECTION

G1: Russian Zelinsky-Kumant respirator, 1916

This sophisticated mask was devised by a professor of chemistry and an engineer. The moulded rubber all-over headpiece incorporated glass (later celluloid) eyepieces, and a nose-like pouch which was used for wiping the eyepieces. The metal filter canister permanently fitted to the facepiece contained bean-sized pieces of activated charcoal – a by-product of vodka manufacture. The respirator suffered from heat build-up and resistance to breathing, and lost its effectiveness owing to the brittleness of the charcoal. The air inlet at the base of the canister was sealed with a cork when not in use, which caused problems when soldiers forgot to remove it during an attack.

G2: French machine-gunner with *Tissot Grande Modèle* respirator, 1917

At the end of 1915 Dr Jules Tissot invented a very effective mask similar to the Large Box Respirator, but using layers of filter materials held in a box on the back, and incorporating a system of drawing air past the eyepieces to keep them clear. It was issued from July 1916 to troops in fixed locations such as machine-gunners and artillery observers. Improvements were made to the box filling in 1917 and 1918. A smaller model was introduced in March 1917.

G3: British horse respirator

The British issued horse respirators from 1916, consisting of a flannelette bag with a canvas mouthpiece; an elastic band held the mouth of the bag around the horse's face, and a flap of calico folded over the bridle noseband to hold it in place. When not in use it was contained in a satchel attached to the bridle. It was less effective than the French and American versions, and was discontinued in the last weeks of the war.

G4: French dog respirator

Based on a photograph, this appears to be a copy of the M2, with eyepieces, an impregnated pad and a waterproof cover.

G5: French *appareil respiratoire spécial*, 1917

The ARS was an advanced mask, but it took over a year to develop. The artillery received it first in March 1917, but universal issue did not take place until February 1918, being completed in May. The facepiece came in three sizes, and the masks were held in cylindrical canisters also containing replacement eyepieces.

H: US ARMY STOKES MORTAR CREW; ST MIHIEL, 12 SEPTEMBER 1918

This 4in Stokes mortar is being operated by men of the 1st Gas Regiment, AEF, at St Mihiel at about 5am on 12 September.

Volunteers from the US 31st Regt of Engineers were attached to the British Special Brigade RE, later forming the 1st Gas Regiment. Six companies each of 300 men were equipped with Stokes mortars and Livens projectors. After the battle of St Mihiel they carried out many small-scale attacks on the Meuse-Argonne front, targeting German rifle and machine-gun positions. They made particularly effective use of the incendiary thermite, air-bursting 50–100ft above German positions. Here, bombs are fired over the heads of the advancing infantry at Zero Hour of the highly successful St Mihiel offensive. The rate of fire was such that crews could fire more than a dozen bombs before the first had exploded. The US-manufactured 'Thermit' rounds (right) have the 12-bore Ballistite blank cartridge propellant in the tail, to which has been added a supplementary ring charge of flake cordite wrapped in cambric. The 'Smoke' projectiles (left) – note yellow band around dirty-white casing – have the later perforated 'cage' tail into which 'biscuits' of propellant were placed, the number depending upon the required range. Both types have the 'Allways' impact detonator, which did not depend on striking nose-first, and which replaced the sprung lever mechanism. The 1st Gas Regt carried M1917 rifles; photographs show no special insignia worn in the field. They have the US-made Small Box Respirator at the 'alert' position on the chest.

INDEX

Figures in **bold** refer to illustrations.